IGNITED
LEGAL
MINDS

Arunoday Devgan

Worldwide Published by

Pendown Press

PENDOWN PRESS LLP
An ISO 9001 & ISO 14001 Certified Co.,
Regd. Office: 3767A, Kanhaiya Nagar,
Tri Nagar, Delhi-110035
Ph.: 8130886000, 9650072927, 8595249536
E-mail: info@pendownpress.com
Branch Office: 1A/2A, 20, Hari Sadan, Ansari Road,
Daryaganj, New Delhi-110002
Ph.: 011-45794768
Website: PendownPress.com

First Edition: 2024
Price: ₹399/-
ISBN: 978-93-5554-774-3

Layout and Cover Designed by Pendown Graphics Team
Printed and Bound in India by Thomson Press India Ltd.

CONTENTS

INTRODUCTION

The legal minds stand as draftsmen of justice, envoys of change, and sentinels of the nation's conscience in the vast and varied terrain of India, amidst the numerous colors of culture, tradition, and history. With their intellectual prowess and unshakable dedication, these inspired legal minds have made a lasting impression on the Indian legal system and society at large. This book sets out on a journey to investigate the lives, contributions, and viewpoints of these individuals. India, a country of contrasts, struggles with the ever-changing web of legal difficulties brought on by its diverse people, complex social structure, and the unrelenting winds of change.

In this evolving landscape, legal minds emerge as guiding lights, interpreting the rules and values that serve as the cornerstone of India's democracy. They make their way through the maze of laws, rulings, and case law, revealing the path to justice and equality.These motivated legal brains have already begun their journey before stepping foot inside the prestigious law school buildings. When children are exposed to the subtleties of right and wrong, fairness and injustice, it frequently begins to take root throughout their formative years. They experience an internal spark that drives them to choose a career path devoted to preserving the law and defending the rights of the populace.

As they traverse this path, the legal minds undergo rigorous legal education, not just to master the intricacies of statutes but also to develop a deep understanding of the legal philosophy that underpins the Constitution of India. They embrace the values of justice, liberty, equality, and fraternity, realizing that these principles are the pillars on which India's democratic edifice stands.

Upon donning the black robes, these ignited legal minds become the vanguards of justice. Whether in bustling metropolitan courts or remote village tribunals, they strive to ensure that every individual, irrespective of their station in life, has equal access to justice. With each case they undertake, they breathe life into the Constitution, shaping the evolution of jurisprudence with their profound insights and thoughtful interpretations.

But the realm of ignited legal minds transcends the boundaries of courtrooms and legal chambers. They venture into the realms of academia, research, and policymaking, actively contributing to the formulation of laws and policies that shape the nation's destiny.

Through their writings, lectures, and public engagements, they participate in the discourse on critical legal and social issues, enriching the national dialogue with their wisdom and erudition. Moreover, these ignited legal minds understand that India's legal landscape cannot be divorced from its social, economic, and political fabric. They are acutely aware of the historical context in which the Indian legal system has evolved and its role in shaping the nation's trajectory. As India confronts contemporary challenges, these legal minds become torchbearers of change, advocating for legal reforms that address the pressing issues of our time.

This book takes you on a fascinating exploration of India's top legal minds, revealing their inspiring stories of success, determination, and resilience. From renowned judges and scholars to influential practitioners, each chapter unveils the remarkable impact these trailblazers have had on shaping India's legal landscape.

We will also be focusing on the aspect of the laws and amendments that have brought a new ignition to our nation's legal policies and societal structures,recognizing that law binds with every structure present or in the past in society.

We will witness the battles fought for justice and equity, the landmark judgments that have reverberated through the annals of history, and the struggles to overcome the barriers that lie in the path of progress.

Come aboard as we explore the fascinating lives of brilliant legal thinkers! We're excited to invite you to celebrate their remarkable intelligence, unwavering commitment, and strength. By learning about their stories, we can better grasp the profound impact these legal luminaries have had on India's history and their ongoing contributions to a more just and equal society.

CHAPTER 1

THE RISE OF INDIAN LEGAL EDUCATION

## 1.	History of Legal Education

In the early part of the 20th century, universities in Kolkata, Madras, Bombay, Delhi, Aligarh, Banaras, and Lucknow built a few full-fledged law colleges. They generated a different breed of legal professionals who could easily qualify as solicitors and be appointed as judges. For a better understanding of the developmental efforts, evaluation panels or commissions were established after gaining independence. The Secondary Education Commission then placed an emphasis on the need for a suitable legal education in 1952–1953, along with a focus on democratic citizenship, professional effectiveness, and personal development. However, the Setalvad Committee, in 1958, observed, "the main purpose of university legal education seems hitherto to have been not the teaching of law as a science or as a branch of learning, but mainly imparting students to a knowledge of certain principles and provisions of law to enable them to enter the legal profession."

As time passed, new needs surfaced, rendering the existing system obsolete and necessitating its replacement. The Education Commission of 1964–1966 advocated for the modernization of society through the arousal of curiosity, but it is obvious that this cannot be accomplished without an effective system of legal education. Therefore, the Review Committee of 1977 advocated for initiatives to shape the student into a citizen as envisioned by the constitution. After adopting the Indian Constitution and its aspirations for human progress, the necessity of high-quality legal education becomes apparent.

The Advocate's Act was passed in 1961 with the intention of regulating the legal profession and enhancing its caliber through the upholding of norms and ethics. This allowed the insertion of procedural learning into the curriculum, aligning legal education with its needs. The ideals in the Preamble of the Constitution served as the foundation for the 1986 Education Policy, which placed particular emphasis on the requirements of the emerging technological society. That was instructed to unite with modernism, spirituality, and technical sophistication. Concurrently, the National Law School of India University, Bangalore, was founded at the same time to offer five-year integrated legal studies. Today, there are 25 National

Law Universities in the country, nurturing mainly the corporate sector, leaving the justice system, as such, starving for talent and quality advocacy.

This means that according to the NEP 2020, "Legal education needs to be competitive globally, adopting best practises and embracing new technologies for wider access to and timely delivery of justice." It correctly emphasizes the need to instill ideals of social, economic, and political justice in legal education while keeping in mind sociocultural context, accessible language, and jurisprudential practice. Actual courtroom experiences and international norms for conciliation, mediation, and arbitration should be part of the experiential learning pattern. The curriculum must include mock exercises covering each area of the legal profession.

The Indian legal school system must place a strong emphasis on producing attorneys who care about the public good for Indian society. By pursuing all of this in accordance with NEP 2020's metrics, the judicial system may be made pleasantly gratifying.

2.   Legal Education Before Independence

Beginning in 1600, the East India Company introduced the British legal system and court procedures. Mayor's Courts were founded by the charters of 1726 and 1753. The Regulating Act of 1773 led to the creation of the Supreme Court of Calcutta in 1774. Governors-general, including Warren Hastings, Cornwallis, Bentinck, etc., implemented a number of judicial changes. During that time, the Barristers travelled from London, and legal education was not present in India.

Access to British Barristers' legal services was limited to only extremely wealthy persons. The demand for Indian advocates was quite high, leading to the launch of legal courses in 1855. Law classes were originally offered in 1855 at the Hindu College in Calcutta, Elphinstone College in Bombay, and Madras. Only men were permitted to enrol in legal classes up to the end of the eighteenth century. It was only in the early 20th century that women started taking legal education courses.

The development of legal education was not adequate until 1947. The length, content, and other aspects of law studies varied greatly from institution to university. There was no consistency. In several universities, graduates plus two years of law school were eligible to receive law degrees. After graduation, the length of the legal programme at certain universities was three years, while in several universities, it was three years after P.U.C. and Matriculation

The primary audience for the law course was legal practitioners, with case laws and related topics making up the majority of the curriculum. These university graduates were interested in working in District Courts, with only a few High Courts in existence, and the Privy Council in London serving as the Highest Appellate Court. Judges accorded English Barristers the utmost respect and regard in the Privy Council and the High Courts. Before English Barristers, Indian solicitors were inferior.

Indians who were interested would travel to England to get a Bar-at-law, which had higher prestige and social standing, after earning a legal degree in India. The "Bar-at-law" degree was valued more highly than a simple LLB from an Indian university; even Gandhiji earned his "Bar-at-law" degree. Until 1961, High Courts had the authority to set the requirements for legal practitioners to be admitted to the bar. The similar condition persisted up to 1961. The Advocates Act, which was passed in 1961, gave the Bar Council of India the authority to specify the legal requirements for admission to the legal profession.

There were innumerable defects in the legal education before independence. The British rulers, perhaps fearing that elevated standards would reflect poorly on their administration, did not aim to develop the education system to their standard.

Professor Arthur Van Mehren wrote -

"The Indian legal profession and legal education were not developed with a rational functional approach to the problems of law and legal order. The Indian legal education inevitably tended to evolve in patterns that emphasized rote memory. To impart information not critical understanding remained the goal of legal education."

3.   Legal Education After Independence

The number of literates has been steadily rising since independence, which has improved the quality of legal education since 1947 and continues now. Legal professionals now have more options for work, including legal roles as legal advisers in industries, Chit Funds, financial businesses, the press, etc., Additionally, there are opportunities for lawyers, judges, professors at law schools, administrators, writers, and reporters. Since 1947, the number of law schools has been steadily increasing.

4.   Role of the Constitution of India in Promoting Legal Education

The Indian Constitution of 1950 gives India a wider perspective on social welfare, political organisation, and economics. It substitutes "social welfare state" for "police state." After independence, a number of High Courts, Tribunals, and lower courts were formed. The Supreme Court of India has replaced the Privy Council as the supreme court. Every person is granted fundamental rights under the Constitution. Now, when a person's basic rights are violated, they can instantly file a lawsuit. The Indian Constitution has expanded understanding of the legal system, economy, social issues, and politics in India.

All of these factors had an impact on legal education. Administrators, lawyers, judges, academics, politicians, and others focused in the advancement of legal education. A number of commissions, committees, etc. were established, and they provided suggestions for the improvement of legal education.

Commission on University Education:

This Commission was founded in 1948. This commission's main goal was to evaluate the standard of higher education. In addition to this main objective, the Commission also inquired about and reported on legal education.

The Commission reported:

"With the attainment of independence and the consequent responsibility of developing our own constitutional government, together with international relations, now as important as domestic affairs, it becomes imperative that we develop high-grade colleges of law, real scholars, and capable of producing individuals who can cope with international, constitutional and administrative problems, as well as with the civil, criminal, and routine demands that exist. Our gifts for philosophical studies would indicate that it is possible to have as great students of systematic law and the principles of jurisprudence as any other people."

5.   Bar Council of India

Based on the report of All India Bar Committee in 1951, the Advocates Act of 1961 was enacted. Subsequently, the Bar Council of India was established in Delhi as a unanimous juristic person.

The Act provides several powers to the Bar Council of India:

a# One of the important powers of the Bar Council of India is that it can lay down standards for legal education in consultation with the universities in India that impart such education and the State Bar Councils (Section 7(I) (h) of the Advocates, Act 1961).

b# Section 7 (I)(i) empowers the Bar Council to recognize universities whose degree in law qualifies for enrolment as an advocate. For this purpose, it can visit and inspect universities or direct the State Bar Councils to do so, following the given directions.

The bold letters in the above section have been newly inserted by the Act 70 of 1993, thereby strengthening the Bar Council's powers over universities and law colleges. Thus, Sections 70(1)(h) and 7(1)(i) give abundant and full powers to the Bar Council to control and manage the universities and law colleges, and thus to improve the standards of the legal education.

 c# Furthermore, Section 49(1)(d) of the Advocates Act, 1961, adds that the Bar Council of India has the general power to make any rules prescribing the standards of legal education to be observed by universities in India and the inspection of universities for that purpose. Section 24(1) of the Advocates Act, 1961, states that a citizen of India will be entitled to be admitted as an advocate if he has obtained a degree in law from a university in India, which is recognised for the purposes of this Act by the Bar Council.

Therefore, the control and management of legal institutions are in the hands of the Bar Council of India. Some universities offer a two-year course called B.G.L. (Bachelor of General Laws), but the Bar Council does not recognize such a course for the purpose of enrolment as an advocate.

CHAPTER 2

GEOPOLITICS & LAW TWO SIDES OF ONE COIN – CHALLENGES / OVERCOME/SOLUTION/ DECLARATION AS G20 PRESIDENCY

1.   Meaning of Geopolitics

Geopolitics,derived from Ancient Greek, is the study of the effects of Earth's geography (both human and physical) on politics and international relations.While geopolitics usually refers to countries and relations between them, it may also extend its focus to two other kinds of states: de facto independent states with limited international recognition and relationships between sub-national geopolitical entities, such as the federal states constituting a federation, confederation, or a quasi-federal system.

On the international relations stage, geopolitics serves as a method for studying foreign policy to understand, explain, and predict international political behaviour through geographical variables. These include area studies, climate, topography, demography, natural resources, and the applied sciences specific to the region being evaluated.

Geopolitics focuses on political power linked to geographic space, in particular, territorial waters and land territory, in correlation with diplomatic history. Topics within geopolitics include relations among the interests of international political actors focused within a given area, space, or geographical element, forming a geopolitical system. Critical geopolitics deconstructs classical geopolitical theories by showing their political and ideological functions for great powers. There are some works that discuss the geopolitics of renewable energy.

According to Christopher Gogwilt and other researchers, the term is currently being used to describe a broad spectrum of concepts, in a general sense used as "a synonym for international political relations", but more specifically "to imply the global structure of such relations." This usage builds on an "early-twentieth-century term for a pseudoscience of political geography" and other pseudoscientific theories of historical and geography determinism.

2. Relation of Geopolitics & Indian Law

The relationship between Indian law and geopolitics is complex and multifaceted, as the legal framework of a nation is deeply intertwined with its geopolitical context. Here are several aspects that illustrate the interplay between Indian law and geopolitics:

1# Territorial Integrity and Sovereignty:

» Geopolitics often revolves around issues of territory, borders, and sovereignty. Indian law, particularly constitutional provisions and statutes, plays a crucial role in defining and safeguarding the territorial integrity of the nation. Legal frameworks address issues related to border disputes, territorial claims, and the protection of sovereign rights.

2# International Relations and Treaties:

» Geopolitics involves the relationships between nations, and these relationships are often governed by international treaties and agreements. Indian law incorporates provisions that enable the country to enter into treaties and international agreements. The implementation and adherence to these agreements are subject to domestic legal considerations.

3# National Security and Defense:

» Geopolitical considerations heavily influence national security policies. Indian law, through acts such as the Armed Forces (Special Powers) Act and others, provides the legal basis for the deployment of the military in certain regions. Legal frameworks are crucial in balancing the need for security with the protection of human rights and civil liberties.

4# Cross-Border Conflicts and Disputes:

» Geopolitical tensions and conflicts can lead to legal disputes, both domestically and internationally. Indian law provides mechanisms for addressing cross-border disputes, whether related to trade, water resources, or human rights. Courts play a vital role in interpreting and applying these laws to resolve conflicts.

5# Human Rights and International Law:

» Geopolitical considerations often intersect with human rights issues. Indian law incorporates international human rights principles, and the judiciary plays a role in interpreting these principles in the context of geopolitical events. Cases

related to refugees, cross-border migrations, and armed conflicts may involve legal considerations informed by international law.

6# Resource Management and Environmental Law:

» Geopolitical considerations influence decisions regarding the exploitation and management of natural resources. Indian environmental laws are designed to balance economic development with ecological sustainability. Geopolitical factors, such as shared river basins or transboundary pollution, may necessitate legal frameworks to address these issues.

7# Global Governance and International Organizations:

» Geopolitical dynamics are reflected in India's engagement with international organizations like the United Nations. Indian law provides the legal basis for participation in global governance structures and compliance with international norms. The decisions and policies formulated at the global level often find expression in domestic legal frameworks.

8# Impact of Geopolitical Shifts on Domestic Legislation:

» Changes in the geopolitical landscape can necessitate adjustments in domestic laws. For example, shifts in alliances or global power structures may lead to the reassessment of trade policies, defense strategies, or diplomatic relations, prompting amendments or new legislation.

Understanding the relationship between Indian law and geopolitics requires an appreciation of the fact that legal frameworks both shape and respond to the geopolitical environment. The legal system acts as a stabilizing force, providing a structured and predictable basis for addressing the challenges and opportunities presented by the ever-changing geopolitical landscape.

3.   Challenges of the Geopolitical Situation for India

Consequences to Consider

◊   Raised Stakes in Kashmir

Increased global cooperation with India, and thus its rise in geopolitical value, comes at potential costs for its neighbour, Pakistan. The most immediate threat is leverage in the Kashmir dispute. Washington's pivot away from Pakistan and towards India is evident in its different levels of engagement with the two South Asian nations. For instance, last year's Independence Day wishes for both countries came from different departments in the US government. For India, the message came directly from US President Joseph R. Biden, reiterating their joint visions in promoting global peace and security. However, for Pakistan, the communication came from US Secretary of State Antony J. Blinken and only emphasized generic, non-defense areas of collaboration, such as student exchanges.

Some may argue that India's rising value vis-à-vis Pakistan is not zero-sum, given that the United States recently defended its military maintenance package to Islamabad. However, this material expression of support appears to be the exception instead of the rule. Messages such as those from former Presidents Barack H. Obama, Donald J. Trump, and today, Joe Biden, have historically been subtle indicators of Washington's aspirations in the region. For instance, Obama called his

2010 Independence Day communications with Pakistan "the expressions of true friendship that come in a time of need." Given the visible contrast today from the previous year, Washington is sending strong signals of India's greater role in the region over Pakistan's.

Diminishing support in Washington in light of India's rising status means that Pakistani leverage in the Kashmir border dispute is at risk now more than ever. Despite recognizing both sides in the Kashmir conflict, the United States has increasingly shown unbalanced support to India. For instance, the US strategy post 2018-border incidents in Kashmir involved hardening its stance on Pakistan's failure to curb terrorism, such as pushing to place the country on a global terrorism financing watch list and suspending military aid. Indeed, the concerns that prompted these actions are well-founded.

However, reports of India's human rights violations in Kashmir from the same time prompted no substantive response from Washington. A year later, when Delhi revoked autonomy for its portion of the disputed Kashmir territory, initiated internet blackouts, put senior political figures on house arrest, and deepened its historic repression of civil society and free expression there, not only did the United States sidestep the issue, but it also welcomed Indian Prime Minister Narendra Modi for a community custom in Houston a month later. Washington's favouritism at the time was evident when Modi was regarded at the summit as "doing a truly exceptional job for India and all the Indian people" by then-President Trump.

Moving to the current day, India's hosting of the G20 in its portion of Kashmir has gone uncriticised by the United States despite Delhi's continued human rights abuses there. Biden even announced plans to host Modi for a state visit in June, in blatant ignorance of reports by the State Department noting increased acts of state repression in India.

Passivity towards India's human rights abuses and destabilizing actions due to its strategic value is hypocritical with regards to the United States purported foreign policy values. It could elicit responses from Islamabad and non-state entities in the region that do not promote stability in South Asia nor are conducive to US interests there. This not only raises the stakes in the Kashmir conflict but also adds a new layer to the region's already tense security architecture.

◊ **Increased Risk of Chinese Retaliation**

By directly jeopardizing China's interests, India's geopolitical ascent has also raised the likelihood of a confrontation between the two countries. Building resilience against Chinese influence in the East and South China Sea, for example, has been the emphasis of Japan's increased engagement and alignment with India. This was made clear by Tokyo's announcement of its new Indo-Pacific strategy in late March, which called on Delhi to provide infrastructure for "maritime warning and surveillance capabilities." India has also steered toward marine security measures with a greater focus on preventing militarization in the disputed zones and safeguarding resource extraction in the Pacific as a result of its strengthening ties with regional allies like Australia. Given Beijing's heavy involvement in these disputed territories, such attempts seem to be singling out China's interests and are bound to push Beijing to retaliate.

The Chinese government has already issued a warning about "conflict and confrontation" in reaction to some of these events. These initiatives, which Beijing views as anti-China, have made India an even more formidable foe with far-reaching possible consequences.

India is shifting its power on border issues with China as a result of its growing importance. For example, recent independent investigations have shown that, in order to provide India with an advantage during a border confrontation in December 2022, the United States supplied vital satellite images of Chinese military deployments. Such combined US-Indian actions, which were reiterated earlier in the year, directly resulted in this intelligence sharing. Joint US-Indian manoeuvres were also conducted in the disputed zone, a month before to these events, in traditionallyclose vicinity to Chinese military bases. Regional analysts caution that "US support for India, while welcomed, must tread carefully so as not to conflate the long-standing India-China border dispute with the recently intensified US-China rivalry."

Washington is expected to keep giving India this kind of strategic support, thus aiding India with its security concerns would probably exacerbate Beijing's resentment of Washington given that Beijing and Washington are already having difficulty coming to a border dispute resolution. Policymakers in the US and other Western countries need to account for this outcome in their calculations.

How is the Region Responding?

In light of these developments, China and Pakistan will modify their strategic calculations in response to these changes, increasing the likelihood of tensions rising and intensifying. China's aggression toward Taiwan is a predictable outcome. Though historically this has been in response to the US, new strategic advances by India put Beijing in more danger. Whether justified or not, China's increased anxieties will affect how forceful it is in the areas it considers to be its own, and the West and the region will need to deal with those changes.

An active indicator of these changes is Beijing's present aggression in the area. China is demonstrating its might in the area by holding "ready to fight" drills near Taiwan and by sending counter-militias to the first-ever ASEAN-Indian joint exercises in the South China Sea. With India and the US working together, it has also directly addressed the concerns associated with border disputes by looking for backing outside. Beijing advocated an exclusive border agreement that might give it more clout with India should it lose crucial territory in the disputed Doklam plateau during reopened negotiations with Bhutan earlier this year. India contests Beijing's attempts to rename a number of locations, and these attempts have been backed by a similar counterreaction strategy. As a result,

Beijing has responded strongly to increased Western pressure on it through India in ways that Washington may not have anticipated.

Pakistan is also anticipated to reaffirm its claim over Kashmir out of concern over the region's declining international significance. Its increasingly assertive position on the matter at the UN is indicative of early indicators. The recent resurgence of disputes between India's and Pakistan's officials over Kashmir during the Shanghai Cooperation Organization summit confirms Pakistan's perception that the international community is not giving its issues enough weight. Relations with its neighbour, India, would only become more unstable if this trend is maintained. Human rights violations and the status change of Kashmir—two concerns for which the US implicitly supports India—have already been highlighted by Islamabad as significant obstacles to a future settlement.

The international community should be extremely cautious given both countries' nuclear weapons, especially in light of Pakistan's growing military and economic connections with China. According to a recent study, Islamabad is currently experiencing internal conflicts on a possible shift towards China (instead of the US). Terrorist attacks have repeatedly brought India and Pakistan to the verge of war. If these rumours are accurate, Pakistan and China may "lock" both the United States and India out of counterterrorism efforts in the region. This poses risks to both countries' national security and the stability of the region.

There may be a possible strategic realignment in that direction, as indicated by the recent trilateral discussions between China, Pakistan, and Afghanistan. Once Washington's pivot to Delhi takes effect and pushes Pakistan firmly into China's camp, the United States and India may soon find it more difficult to confront counterterrorism and similar regional concerns that are already returning.

Political and Economic Crises in Sri Lanka

The ongoing crisis in Sri Lanka are a significant concern in the area. India extended its support by providing gasoline, medications, and humanitarian goods, relaxing its purse strings more than any other country in such a short period.

Delhi, the capital of India, is also helping the island nation in securing an IMF deal to lower its debt. Due to China being a rival in Sri Lanka, Delhi seeks a government that is conscious of India's security and strategic interests.

Engagement with Russia

The border stalemate with China has highlighted India's strategic reliance on Russia.

Moscow has been a trustworthy provider of defence equipment for the past 70 years and continues to be the market leader, despite diversification to include the US, France, and Israel, among others. This has become more difficult as a result of the crisis between Russia and Ukraine, which has increased strain on the supply chain and raised questions about the dependability of Russian equipment.

Neighbourhood Challenges

Sri Lanka will continue to demand India's political, financial, and humanitarian attention in the upcoming year, while New Delhi will be a topic of political conversation in the Maldives. In September, the Maldives will have elections, and an "India Out" campaign is anticipated to incite contentious political debate. Delhi will keep a close eye on political parties' attempts to portray India as a bully and a big brother.

Relationship with the West

With India sticking to its plan of buying cheaper oil and staying neutral regarding Russia, it now needs to reassure its Western friends, like Europe and the United States.

Pakistan

Looking to recent events, the 2024 Pakistani elections have concluded, marking a pivotal moment in the relationship between India and Pakistan. The outcome of these elections will play a crucial role in determining the trajectory of bilateral relations and regional stability in the coming years.

Their perception of India will be shaped by the Army commander and the next civilian government. The relationship's future in India, where the Lok Sabha elections are set for 2024, may hinge on how the Pakistan issue is handled.

Sri Lanka and Maldives

◊ While Sri Lanka will continue to demand India's humanitarian, financial and political attention in 2024, India will also be part of the political conversation in the Maldives.

◊ The Maldives is heading to the polls in September 2023, and an "India Out" campaign is likely to fire up the political debate. Delhi will be watching closely as political parties try to project India as a bully and a big brother.

Bangladesh

◊ Bangladesh is also entering election mode in 2023, with polls scheduled for January 2024 after the iron-fisted reign of Sheikh Hasina.

◊ India will be looking at her prospects after a long and uninterrupted political journey that has brought security to India's eastern states.

Nepal

◊ Events in Nepal took a dramatic turn when former rebel-turned-politician Pushpa Kamal Dahal, known as "Prachanda," was appointed Prime Minister, and former Prime Minister K P Oli, a well-known India-baiter in recent years, was given control of the government.

India will face a big challenge due to Beijing's growing sway in Kathmandu in recent years.

4. India's Solution to these Geopolitical Challenges

Moving Forward

In general, one cannot only see India's ascent through the prism of Delhi's increasing prominence on the world stage. The key issue is how China and Pakistan perceive threats which might destabilize the area, whether they are real or not. Those in the international community who are starting to view India more highly as a geopolitical anchor need to be mindful of these ramifications. The security architecture of the region will not shift exclusively to India's advantage, as the US and its allies had hoped. Conflict dynamics and security realignments may present more opportunities for conflict escalation and confrontation if Pakistan and China proceed to strengthen their relations in response.

Talking about clarifying intentions and reducing feelings of threat might be beneficial in the near run. Long-term communication with Middle Eastern allies like Saudi Arabia and the United Arab Emirates will be a helpful vantage point. Keeping an eye on regional dynamics, these nations have managed to sustain growing collaboration with China, India, and Pakistan at the same time. Mutual trust between these parties, notwithstanding differences in intensity, may be able to ease tensions, particularly those between Pakistan and India that have been rumoured.

In the long term, the United States should continue to deepen ties with India if this aligns with its foreign policy objectives, but it must also engage meaningfully with other regional stakeholders. This balancing act will require more than just passively "monitoring" India's human rights violations. The U.S. must call out such repressive acts, particularly against Muslim minorities, to convey its impartiality on Kashmir. Using its leverage with Delhi to address these and other issues will reduce the risk of escalation with Pakistan, which will respond (whether productively or not) to stay relevant in the Kashmir conversation. Likewise, pressure on Beijing through India should be pursued with caution, taking into account. China's potential responses elsewhere, such as in Taiwan and maritime disputes where it continues to assert strength.

Ultimately, there will probably still be a lot of strife in the region. However, the West, whether it is applying pressure on China or combating terrorism, can effectively moderate the escalation by pursuing its aims while considering the long-term effects of its actions.

Putting India's Rise in Context

India's growing geopolitical significance in the West and throughout the region is indicative of its ascent. For example, the US and India have closer connections now than ever before. From now on, the two have come to see themselves as "two pillars of a free and open Indo-Pacific." Numerous new alliances in vital defense sectors, many of which were started by the US, attest to this increase in strategic significance. This growing relevance is reinforced by US Secretary of Defense Lloyd J. Austin III's description of these collaborative activities with India as "operating and coordinating more closely together than ever."

India's growing influence in the region is consistent with this trend. Although Indo-Japanese relations have always been good, since last year they have achieved significant progress together. Japan and India convened in September of last year to extend their combined military exercises. The Japanese foreign minister described their security cooperation as "expanding drastically." Talks about stepped-up defense cooperation measures were also held with Thailand last month. Invitations to important security discussions—like the Pacific leaders meet-up, which was initially set for May 21–22 and to which only India and the United States were invited—highlight India's ascent in the geopolitical architecture of the area. Prime Minister James Marape of Papua New Guinea and other regional organizers referred to the gathering as a "futuristic meeting of global superpowers" when they announced it, which further contributed to the increased awareness of India's growing importance.

Observers in the area should be concerned about these trends for two reasons. First, they are timely given the status of the globe today, and second, they are expanding in nature. India's growing importance has emerged mostly from defense alliances. Building a more robust and varied defense architecture with Delhi has been the main focus for those who believe India's strategic worth is increasing, notwithstanding other areas of cooperation, such as the economic front.

When combined with its timing, the necessity for prudence about increasing defense cooperation becomes evident. This coincides with heightened Western concerns about Taiwan for China. Following the withdrawal of US forces from Afghanistan and the impending political and economic turmoil in Pakistan, these developments have less significance now. China and Pakistan face greater challenges as a result of India's growing significance to both the West and its regional allies. China wants to keep its grip on Taiwan, and Pakistan wants to keep control over Kashmir. However, India's growing might could jeopardize these interests and their ability to use strategic

leverage in territorial conflicts.

In an area already beset by what the US Institute of Peace refers to as a "cascading security dilemma" involving three nuclear-armed nations (China, India, and Pakistan), the international community runs the risk of entering treacherous geopolitical waters without taking the larger ramifications of its decisions into account.

> ***"Europe has to grow out of the mindset that its problems are the world's problems, but the world's problems are not Europe's problems."***

German Chancellor Olaf Scholz cited Indian Minister of External Affairs Subrahmanyam Jaishankar's audacious remarks at the GLOBSEC Bratislava Forum 2022 at the Munich Security Conference in 2023. Notably, the latter requote was made just prior to the one-year anniversary of the conflict between Russia and Ukraine, and it came from a crucial Western representative, Germany. India is at the forefront of geopolitics, from its G20 leadership to the US, including Delhi, in its Indo-Pacific security strategy. It is becoming more strategically important to the West. Views in the region are also beginning to change in its favor: important alliances like the Association of Southeast Asian Nations (ASEAN) are growing their alliances with India and actively seeking out Delhi's collaboration.

These developments might not seem like much when taken alone. However, other significant regional actors like China and Pakistan have suffered as a result of India's increasing geopolitical significance. Regrettably, international policymakers are not giving these effects more thought. China and Pakistan will respond by modifying their strategic calculi to safeguard their interests and relevance in the West and the region.Hence, a deeper understanding of these events is necessary to enable the international community to make well-informed judgments when interacting with India and Asia.

Although not a zero-sum game, India's increased geopolitical clout could worsen regional tensions rather than ease them if the international community embraces it without question. Thus, there is a significant chance that Western objectives for a "free and open Indo-Pacific," as envisioned by those who are increasingly looking to India for support, may backfire.

5. India's Declaration as President of G20

The New Delhi G20 Leaders' Declaration, which was overwhelmingly approved by all G20 nations on the first day of the summit, served as the summit's main focal point. It is an ambitious, inclusive, decisive, and action-oriented declaration that lays out the path forward on a number of pressing global issues. This marks a significant turning point in India's quest to take its due place among nations. The 83 paragraphs were all agreed upon. The highlights of it were:

◊ Adopted a consensus-driven approach that aligned with national viewpoints in addressing the geopolitical issue of the conflict in Ukraine.

◊ Advocated for the Global South's voice and welcomed the African Union as a member.

◊ Dedicated to carrying out the G20 2023 Action Plan to Quicken SDG Progress.

◊ Endorsed LiFE, our concept for nudging pro-planet behaviouralchanges.

◊ Increased funding for development and climate change from billions to trillions of dollars.

◊ Agreed to establish a New Collective Quantified Goal (NCQG) for Climate Finance in 2024 that is clear, aggressive, and trackable, starting at a floor of USD 100 billion annually.

◊ Larger, better, more efficient, and more representative MDBs were demanded.

◊ Defined, finalized its framework, and approved Digital Public Infrastructure to provide large-scale, reasonably priced services.

◊ The Green Development Pact aims to achieve inclusive, sustainable, balanced, and integrated economic growth.

◊ Said that by 2030, renewable energy would be tripled worldwide.

◊ Agreed to expedite the production of zero- and low-emission hydrogen, as well as to create worldwide markets and international standards for it.

◊ Agreed on women-led development, with the goal of halving the gender digital divide by 2030 and enabling their full, equal, and effective participation as decision-makers.

◊ Dedicated to improving the world's food security and supporting the millet research initiative.

◊ Endorsed a Global Initiative on Digital Health for Universal HealthCoverage.

◊ The WHO Center in Jamnagar stated that traditional medicine has a recognized function.

◊ Denounced terrorism in all its manifestations and emphasized the refusal of refuge.

◊ Stressed responsible AI with pro-innovation governance and regulation.

◊ Supported frequent, skill-based, and well-managed migration channels.

India's footprint was seen in G20 Outcome Documents, as follows:

◊ The Deccan High-Level Principles of Nutrition and Food Security

◊ High-Level Principles of the Chennai Blue/Ocean Economy

◊ The Tourism Roadmap of Goa

◊ The implementation roadmap for land restoration in Gandhinagar

◊ A call to action in Jaipur to improve MSMEs

◊ The Kansai Culture Trail

New initiatives during India's G20 Presidency were:

◊ Group for Disaster Risk Reduction

◊ Startup20 Participation Group

◊ Roundtable of Chief Scientific Advisors

◊ G20 Meeting on Law Enforcement and Security in the Era of NFTs, AI, and the Metaverse

◊ A new working group on women's empowerment (agreed)

◊ Collaboration in the fight against drugs

◊ Collaboration in the field of traditional medicine

◊ The initiative for millet research

Achievements on the sidelines of the G20 Summit were as follows:

» **Launch of Global Biofuel Alliance (GBA):**

Initiating countries -Argentina, Brazil,India, Italy, Mauritius, South Africa, UAE and USA;

Observers: Canada, Bangladesh and Singapore

» **India-Middle East-Europe Economic Corridor (IMEC):**

Signatories -India, SaudiArabia, UAE, USA, EU Commission, France, Italy andGermany

» **India-Brazil-South Africa-USA meeting:**

The current (India) and 3 incoming(Brazil, South Africa and USA) G20 Presidencies' meeting committedto build bigger, better, and moreeffective MDBs together with theWorld Bank.

» **Partnership for Global Infrastructure and Investment (PGI):**

Participants were India, USA, Saudi Arabia, UAE, EU, Italy, France,Germany, Japan, Mauritius and World Bank. Under the PGI, the G7aims to mobilize US$ 600 billion by 2027in global infrastructureinvestments, including in partnership with the private sector, and forachievement of SDGs. PGI projects in India include those inthe health, telecom and renewable energy sectors.

India's Contribution to the G20

India's Presidency imparted a new dynamism and momentum to the G20, and built consensus on a wide range of issues among developing countries and advanced economies. India brought multilateralism back to the centre stage and amplified the voice of the Global South. India will continue to stay fully engaged in the G20 in the future.

CHAPTER 3

ELEVEN IMPORTANT AMENDMENTS THAT CHANGED INDIAN LEGAL SYSTEM AND PROVISION OF ARTICLE 370

1.   First Amendment Act 1951

The formal name of the amendment is the Constitution (First Amendment) Act, 1951. The motion was made on May 10 of that year by Jawaharlal Nehru, the Prime Minister of India at the time, and it was approved by Parliament on June 18 of the same year.

This Amendment set a precedent for amending the Constitution to overcome court rulings that limited the government's ability to implement certain policies and programmes.

The Fundamental Rights provisions of the Indian Constitution were modified in a number of ways by the 1951 Constitution (First Amendment) Act. It provided strategies for restricting free speech and expression, backed initiatives to eliminate zamindari, and made it clear that the principle to equality does not prevent lawmakers from introducing legislation that provides "particular consideration" to society's most disadvantaged groups.

It was stated in the Statement of Reasons (SOR) for the First Amendment that "Challenges to agrarian laws or laws relating to land reform were pending in courts and were holding up large schemes of land legislation through dilatory and wasteful litigation."

◊ The First Amendment Act amended articles 15, 19, 85, 87, 174, 176, 341, 342, 372, and 376.

◊ It also provided for the saving of laws providing for the acquisition of estates.

◊ Added three more grounds of restrictions on freedom of speech and expression-public order, friendly relations with foreign states, and incitement to an offense. Also, it made the restrictions 'reasonable' and thus, justiciable.

- ◊ Provided that state trading and nationalization of any trade or business by the state are not to be invalid on the grounds of violation of the right to trade or business.

- ◊ It introduced the Ninth Schedule to protect the land reforms and other laws included in it from Judicial Review.

- ◊ Articles 31A and 31B were inserted after Article 31.

What led to the amendment?

The need to restrict freedom of expression arose in 1950 after the government received heavy press criticism for its reaction to the refugee inflow in West Bengal and the arbitrary murders of communist dissidents in Madras. The government attempted to censor the media, but the courts determined that this was illegal, forcing the administration to come up with another plan of action.

The provisions of Article 31 state that the legislation specified in the Ninth Schedule cannot be challenged in court because they violated the fundamental rights of citizens. Under Article 31(A), the State now has broad jurisdiction to acquire estates or take over the management of any firm or property that serves the public interest. It sought to prevent judicial review of such transactions under Articles 14 and 19 by doing so.

The Ninth Schedule was often misused. It contains a list of more than 250 legislation that are exempt from judicial scrutiny.

Articles 31(A), 31(B), and 31(C) kept land reform regulations in place and gave priority to the execution of the Directive Principles above individual liberties, despite the Supreme Court's decision in the Kesavananda Bharti Cases of 1973 that judicial review cannot be eliminated as a basic structure.

Statement of Objects and Reasons:

Several issues have come to light during the previous fifteen months of the Constitution's operation as a result of court rulings and announcements, particularly in relation to the chapter on basic rights. According to certain courts, the freedom of speech and expression granted by Article 19(1)(a) of the constitution does not make a person liable, even if they support violent acts like murder. Freedom of speech and the press are not seen as prohibiting the State from punishing or preventing misuse of these rights in other nations with codified constitutions.

The right of a citizen to engage in any vocation, trade, or business under Article 19(1)g is subject to reasonable limitations that may be imposed by the state's laws "in the interests of the general public." Although the wording is broad enough to include any nationalisation programme the state may implement, it is nonetheless preferable to clarify the issue by amending Article 19(6). Another article 31 that has encountered unforeseen issues is Article 31.

Despite the provisions of clauses (4) and (6) of Article 31, the validity of the agrarian reform laws passed by state legislatures over the past three years has become the subject of protracted litigation, causing the delay in implementing these crucial laws that will significantly impact on a large number of people.

The major goals of this bill are to completely secure the constitutional legality of zamindari abolition legislation in general and a few specific State Acts in particular, by amending Article 19 as outlined above. The opportunity has been taken to propose some modest changes to other articles in order to resolve any issues.

According to Article 46, the State shall take special care to advance the educational and economic interests of the poorer segments of the population and safeguard them from social injustice.It establishes this as a guiding principle of State policy. It is suggested that Article 15(3) be appropriately extended so that any special provisions the State may make for the educational, economic, or social progress of any disadvantaged class of people may not be contested on the grounds of being discriminatory.

The Bill also includes essential adjustments regarding sections that deal with calling and proroguing Parliamentary sessions. Additionally, there are a few minor amendments in respect of Articles 341, 342, 372 and 376.

2.   The Constitution (7th amendment) Act, 1956

Statement Of Objects and Reasons:

In order to implement the scheme of States reorganisation, it is necessary to make numerous amendments in the Constitution, effective from October 1, 1956. This bill seeks to enact these amendments and make additionalchanges to certain provisions of the Constitution related to the High Courts and High Court Judges, the executive power of the Union and the States, and a few entries in the legislative lists. The reasons for making these amendments are indicated below:-

- ◊ **Clause 2:-** The reorganisation scheme involves not only the establishment of new States and alterations in the area and boundaries of the existing States but also the abolition of the three categories of States (Part A, Part B and Part C States) and the classification of certain areas as Union territories. Article 1 has to be suitably amended for this purpose, and the First Schedule completely revised.

◊ **Clause 3:-** The changes that are suggested in Article 80 are official and direct. The Fourth Schedule to the Constitution, which determines how the seats in the Council of States are distributed among the existing States, must be completely revised to accommodate the geographical changes and the creation of new states and Union territories, as suggested in Part II of the States Reorganisation Bill, 1956. The current distribution is based on the population of each State as determined by the census taken in 1941. One seat is allocated to each Part A and Part B State for the first five million, and one seat for every additional two million or portion thereof that exceeds one million. It is suggested that the seat distribution be changed, albeit using the same method, based on the results of the most recent census.

◊ **Clause 4:-** Comprehensive amendments to Articles 81 and 82 are required due to the abolishment of Part C States in their original form and the creation of Union territories. Article 81(1)(b)'s directive that "the States shall be divided, grouped or formed into territorial constituencies" will no longer be applicable because, following the reorganisation, each State will be large enough to be divided into a number of constituencies and will not be able to be "formed" into a single territorial constituency or "grouped" with other States for this purpose.

To provide appropriate provisions for Union territories, Clause (2) of Articles 81 and 82 must be integrated and updated. It is suggested that the articles be revised and simplified rather than being altered in pieces. In addition, it is suggested to set a limit on the total number of representatives that Parliament may designate for the Union territory in Clause (1)(b) of the new article 81.

- ◊ **Clause 5:-** The elimination of Part B States has consequences for the proposed amendment of the proviso to Article 131. The existing proviso's two sections have been consolidated.

- ◊ **Clause 6:-** According to Article 153, each State shall have a Governor. It is suggested that a proviso be added to this article to remove any potential technical obstacles to the nomination of a Governor for two or more States, as doing so may be beneficial under certain conditions.

- ◊ **Clause 7:-** Bi-cameral legislatures are permitted in several States under sub-paragraph (a) of Clause (1) of Article 168. It is suggested that such a legislative be established in the expanded Madhya Pradesh, as well as continuing to exist in the reorganised States of Punjab and Mysore. Since it would take time to establish a Legislative Council for Madhya Pradesh, it is suggested that the applicable adjustment to Article 168(1)(a) be put into effect at a later date through a President-issued public notification.

◊ **Clause 8:-** This seeks to revise Article 170 mainly with a view to bringing it into line with Articles 81 and 82 as revised by Clause 4.

◊ **Clause 9: -** The maximum size of the Legislative Council of a State is set at one-fourth of the size of the Legislative Assembly of such State under Clause (1) of Article 171. Although this amount is appropriate in larger States like Uttar Pradesh and Bihar, it causes problems for smaller States. Therefore, it is recommended to change the maximum to one-third of the Legislative Assembly's membership.

◊ **Clause 10:-** According to Article 216, the President is able to appoint as many judges to a High Court as deemed necessary from time to time and set the maximum number of judges for each High Court by a separate decree. Practically speaking, the proviso has limited meaning because the President can always alter the order establishing the maximum. The appointment of extra and acting judges for which Clause 14 seeks to make provision will likewise need frequent changes to the order or a large number being set as the maximum. Therefore, it is suggested that Article 216 be amended to remove the proviso.

◊ **Clause 11:-** The amendment of Clause (1) of Article 217 proposed in this clause is consequential to the proposal to provide for the appointment of additional and acting judges for limited periods.

◊ **Clause 12:-** Article 220's complete ban on practising law after retiring from the court has a significant impact on how High Court justices are chosen from the bar. The article is being amended to soften this strict prohibition and allow retired judges to practise in the Supreme Court and any High Court other than the one where they previously served as permanent judges.

◊ **Clause 13:-** The President is given the authority to move judges from one High Court to another under Article 222. According to Clause (2) of this article, when a judge is so moved, he is entitled to earn a compensation payment in addition to his salary. Since it is believed that there is no genuine rationale for giving such an exemption, it is suggested that Clause (2) be removed.

◊ **Clause 14:-** It has been determined that the Article 224 provision allowing retired judges to be called back for brief stints on the High Court bench is neither sufficient nor suitable. Therefore, it is suggested that this article be replaced with a clause that allows for the appointment of extra judges to make up for backlogs as well as the appointment of acting judges to fill temporary vacancies.

◊ **Clause 15:-** With consideration for the post-reorganisation constitutional situation of States and Union territories, it is recommended to modify and simplify Articles 230, 231, and 232. While each State will typically have a distinct High Court under Article 214, the authority to create joint High Courts for two or more

States will be necessary. Additionally, authority will be needed to both include and exclude a Union territory from a High Court's jurisdiction, depending on the situation. These provisions will be made by the updated articles 230 and 231.

◊ **Clause 16:-** The administration of Part C States is outlined in Part VIII of the Constitution, and the administration of Part D territory is outlined in Part IX. It is suggested to remove Part IX and revise Part VIII to address the management of Union territory.

◊ **Clause 17:-** While article 258 (1) gives the President the authority to delegate Union activities to a State Government or its officials, there is no analogous clause allowing a state's governor to delegate State duties to the Central Government or its deputies. This gap has been discovered to have a practical impact on how some development programmes are carried out in the United States. It is suggested that a new article 258A be added to cover the gap.

◊ **Clause 18:-** Travancore's obligation to continue making an annual contribution of Rs. 51 lakhs to the Travancore Devaswom Fund was spelled out in Article VIII of the Covenant signed by the Rulers of Travancore and Cochin in May 1949 for the creation of the United State of Travancore and Cochin.

The Constitution's article 238(10)(ii) affirmed this system. It is suggested that the current arrangement should continue even after the creation of the new State of Kerala, but that the contribution from the Consolidated Fund of that State to the Travancore Devaswom Board should be decreased from Rs. 51 lakhs to Rs. 46.5 lakhs in light of the transfer of territory from Travancore-Cochin to Madras.

◊ **Clause 19:-** It is proposed to revise and broaden the scope of Article 298 in this clause, primarily to clarify that both the Union Government and the State Governments have the authority to conduct any commercial or industrial undertaking, regardless of whether it relates to a subject falling under the legislative purview of the Union or, as the case may be, of the State. Similar to this, the Union or a State may hold, purchase, sell, and enter into contracts for any reason without violating the constitution. At the same time, the revised article provides that this extended executive power of the Union and of the States will be subject, in the former case, to legislation by the State, and in the latter case, to legislation by Parliament.

◊ **Clause 20:-** The new Article 350A proposed in this clause is designed to implement one of the States Reorganisation Commission's important recommendations regarding safeguards for linguistic minorities in the States after reorganisation.

◊ **Clause 21:-** It is suggested that Article 371 be replaced by a different article that makes particular provisions for the States of Andhra and Punjab. Through appropriate changes to the government rules of business and the rules of procedure of the Assembly, this item will give the President the ability to create regional committees of the State Legislative Assembly and ensure their proper operation.

◊ **Clause 22:-** From the designated day forward, the High Court of Travancore-Cochin will serve as the High Court for the newly created State of Kerala, while the High Courts of Mysore and Rajasthan will continue to serve as the High Courts for the expanded "new" States bearing those titles, respectively. It is believed that there is no need to raise the wages paid to the Judges of these High Courts to the level of the other High Courts, taking into account the level of revenue at the bar and salaries payable to the judicial services in these States.

It is suggested to change sub-paragraph (1) of paragraph 10 of the Second Schedule to the Constitution, which currently pays the Chief Justices of these three High Courts a salary of Rs. 3,000 and the other Judges a compensation of Rs. 2,500. Occasionally, a retired district judge must be appointed as a High Court judge. It has been standard policy to get from him an agreement that he would not make a pension claim while serving as a High Court judge because there is no legal mechanism for withholding the pension owed to such a judge. Since this is obviously unsatisfactory, it is proposed to add a proviso to paragraph 10(1) of the Second Schedule on the same lines as the proviso to paragraph 9(1) thereof regulating the salary of a judge of the Supreme Court in similar circumstances.

Sub-paragraphs (3) and (4) of paragraph 10 are no longer required since appropriate provision has been made in the High Court Judges (Conditions of Service) Act, 1954.

◊ **Clause 23:-** There are unnecessarily complex technical issues with law as a result of the three items in the legislative lists (numbers 33 in List I, 36 in List II, and 42 in List III) that all deal with the government's purchase and requisitioning of property. It is suggested to remove the entries from the Union and State List and replace the item from the Concurrent List with a comprehensive entry covering the entire subject in order to prevent these issues and simplify the constitutional situation.

◊ **Clause 24:-** Ancient and historical monuments and documents, as well as archaeological sites and remnants, are referred to as items of national interest in entry 67 of the Union List. An Act of Parliament designated several historical structures, archaeological sites, etc. as being of national significance. The process looks too complicated and calls for another Act of Parliament to make even the smallest additions or changes to the lists in that Act.

Therefore, it is suggested that the entry be changed to read "declared by or under law made by Parliament" instead of "declared by Parliament by law". The associated provisions, entry 12 of the State List, entry 40 of the Concurrent List, and Article 49, are all planned to have the same modification.

◊ **Clause 25:-** The Union List contains two items, 7 and 52, related to industries, although entry 24 of List II only mentions entry 52. This provision aims to correct the apparent oversight that led to the omission of entry 7 of List I.

◊ **Clause 26 and the Schedule:-** These include the consequences, minor changes, and repeals that the Constitution (Removal of Difficulties) Order No. VIII and the Constitution (Removal of Difficulties) Order No. VIII, applicable to the Assam tribal territories, are planned to make.

3.   The Constitution (24th amendment) Act, 1971

Statement of Objects and Reasons:

In the well-known Golak Nath case [1967, 2 S.C.R. 762], the Supreme Court narrowly overturned its own prior rulings affirming Parliament's jurisdiction to change all provisions of the Constitution, including Part III, which deals with basic rights. As a result of the ruling, it is believed that Parliament lacks the authority to remove or limit any of the fundamental rights protected by Part III of the Constitution, even if doing so becomes necessary for carrying out the Directive Principles of State Policy and achieving the goals outlined in the Preamble to the Constitution.

Therefore, it is deemed necessary to explicitly state that Parliament has the authority to alter any provision of the Constitution to bring the provisions of Part III within the purview of that power.

The Bill makes it plain that Article 368 allows for alteration of the Constitution as well as the method thereof, and it attempts to change article 368 appropriately for this purpose. The Bill further stipulates that the President must provide his/her consent when a Constitution Amendment Bill that has been approved by both Houses of Parliament is brought to him for approval. The Bill also aims to change Article 13 of the Constitution so that it no longer applies to any amendments made in accordance with Article 368.

4.   The Constitution (42nd Amendment) Act, 1976

Statement of Objects and Reasons appended to the Constitution (Forty-fourth Amendment) Bill, 1976 (Bill No. 91 of 1976) which was enacted as THE CONSTITUTION (Forty-second Amendment) Act, 1976.

Statement of Objects and Reasons:

1# For a constitution to be alive, it must develop. The Constitution will virtually atrophy if the barriers preventing its expansion are not eliminated. In recent years, the government and the general public have been actively focusing on the issue of amending the Constitution to address the challenges that have emerged in achieving the goal of a socioeconomic revolution, aiming to end poverty, ignorance, disease, and opportunity inequality.

2# The democratic institutions outlined in the Constitution are generally good, and criticising any of them is not the way to advance. There is no denying that these institutions have faced significant pressures and strains, and special interests have sought to further their own interests at the great cost of the common good.

3# Therefore, it is proposed to amend the Constitution to make the directive principles more comprehensive and to give them precedence over those fundamental rights, which have sometimes been used as an excuse to thwart socio-economic reforms for implementing the directive principles. This will expressly state the high ideals of socialism, secularism, and the integrity of the nation. Additionally, it is suggested that the basic responsibilities of citizens be outlined, and that specific rules be established to deal with any anti-national activity, whether it be carried out by individuals or organisations.

4# The core of democracy is that the will of the people should triumph, and Parliament and State Legislatures represent that desire. Even though the all-inclusive character of the amending authority is explicitly stated in article 368 of the Constitution, it is considered important to make this point clear. By establishing requirements for the minimum number of judges to decide on constitutionality claims and a special majority of at least two-thirds to declare any law unconstitutional, the proposalaims to strengthen the presumption in favour of the constitutionality of legislation passed by Parliament and State Legislatures. To avoid the proliferation of proceedings regarding the constitutional validity of the same Central law in different High Courts and the ensuing possibility that the Central law would be valid in one State but invalid in another State, it is also proposed to remove the jurisdiction of High Courts concerning the determination of constitutional validity of Central laws and grant exclusive jurisdiction in this regard to the Supreme Court.

5# It is deemed necessary to create administrative and other tribunals to handle such matters while maintaining the Supreme Court's jurisdiction over them under Article 136 of the Constitution.This is to reduce the mounting backlog of cases in High Courts and ensure the swift resolution of service matters, revenue matters, and other matters of particular importance in the context of socioeconomic development and progress. Additionally, some adjustments must be made to the High Courts' Article 226 writ jurisdiction.

6# It is proposed to avail of the present opportunity to make certain other amendments which have become necessary in the light of the working of the Constitution.

7# The various amendments proposed in the Bill have been explained in the notes on clauses.

The Bill seeks to achieve the above objects.

5. The Constitution (52nd Amendment) Act, 1985

Statement of Objects and Reasons appended to the Constitution (Fifty-second Amendment) Bill, 1985 (Bill No. 22 of 1985) which was enacted as THE CONSTITUTION (Fifty-second Amendment) Act, 1985.

Statement of Objects and Reasons:

Political defections are detrimental and have been a topic of national concern. If not stopped, the core foundations of our democracy and the values that support it are likely to be threatened. To address this issue, it was promised in the President's Address to Parliament that the Government would present an anti-defection Bill during the current legislative session. This Bill is intended to make defection illegal and fulfill the promise made above.

The bill aims to change the Constitution to state that an elected member of Parliament or a State Legislature, who was chosen by a political party as a candidate, and a nominated member of Parliament or a State Legislature, who is a member of a political party at the time he assumes his seat or who becomes a member of a political party within six months of doing so, would be disqualified on the basis of defection if they voluntarily renounce their membership in that party.

A member of the State Legislature or the Parliament who is independent and joins a political party after being elected is also ineligible. A candidate for election to the House of Commons or the State Legislature, who was not a member of a political party at the time of his nomination and who had not joined one before the passing of six months after being sworn in, will be disqualified if he does so after the expiration of the allotted six months.

The Bill also includes appropriate procedures for political party fusions and splits. A unique clause has been included in the Bill to allow the presiding officer of a House who has been elected to break ties with his or her political party. The presiding officer of the House will decide whether a member of a House of Parliament or State Legislature has become subject to the proposed disqualification. If the question relates to the presiding officer himself, a member of the House will be chosen by the House to make that decision.

The Bill seeks to achieve the above objects.

6.   The Constitution (61st Amendment) Act, 1988

Statement of Objects and Reasons appended to the Constitution (Sixty-second Amendment) Bill, 1988 (Bill No. 129 of 1988) which was enacted as THE CONSTITUTION (Sixty-first Amendment) Act, 1988.

Statement of Objects and Reasons:

In accordance with Article 326 of the Constitution, voters must be at least 21 years old to be eligible to vote in elections for the House of the People and the Legislative Assembly of each State. It has been observed that many nations have set the voting age at 18 years old. In our nation, a few state governments have set an election age of 18 for local government positions. Today's young people are educated and informed, and decreasing the voting age would provide the country's underrepresented youth anopportunity to express their opinions and become involved in politics. The present-day youth are very much politically conscious. Therefore, it is proposed to reduce the voting age from 21 years to 18 years.

The Bill seeks to achieve the above object.

7. The Constitution (73rd Amendment) Act, 1992

Statement of Objects and Reasons:

Despite the fact that the Panchayati Raj Institutions have been in existence for a while, it has been noted that they have not been able to achieve the status and dignity of viable and responsive people's bodies for several reasons.These include the lack of regular elections, protracted supersession, inadequate representation of weaker groups like women and Scheduled Castes and Tribes, insufficient devolution of power, and a lack of financial resources.

According to Article 40 of the Constitution, which is one of the Directive Principles of State Policy, the State shall make efforts to create village panchayats and grant them the essential authorities and authority to act as self-governing bodies. To provide Panchayati Raj Institutions with certainty, continuity, and strength, it is considered that it is urgently necessary to enshrine certain fundamental and essential features of Panchayati Raj Institutions in the Constitution.This is in light of experience over the past forty years and considering the shortcomings that have been observed.

As a result, it is suggested that a new Part dealing with Panchayats be added to the Constitution.This new part aims, among other things, to provide for the Gram Sabha in a village or group of villages, establish Panchayats at the village level and/or other levels, conduct direct elections for all seats in

Panchayats at the village and intermediate levels, as well as for Panchayat Chairpersons at such levels.It also proposes the reservation of seats for the Scheduled Castes and Scheduled Tribes in proportion to their numbers,ensuring that women must occupy at least one-third of the seats, establishing a 5-year term for Panchayats, and mandating elections within six months if a Panchayat is superseded.

Other provisions include disqualifications from Panchayat membership, devolution of authority and accountability from the State Legislature to the Panchayats for creating plans for social justice and economic development, as well as the execution of development initiatives. Panchayats can maintain good financial operations by obtaining state legislature approval for grants from the state's consolidated fund and assigning or appropriating revenues from designated taxes, duties, tolls, and fees.The proposal also suggests setting up a Finance Commission within one year of the proposed amendment and thereafter, every 5 years, to review the financial position of Panchayats, auditing the accounts of the Panchayats,granting powers to State Legislatures to make provisions with respect to elections to Panchayats under the superintendence, direction, and control of the chief electoral officer of the State.

The application of the provisions of the said Part to Union territories, excluding certain States and areas from the application of the provisions of the said Part, the continuance of existing laws and Panchayats until one year from the commencement of the proposed amendment, and barring interference by courts in electoral matters relating to Panchayats are also part of the proposed changes.

The Bill seeks to achieve the aforesaid objectives.

8.   The Constitution (86th Amendment) Act, 2002

1# Article 45 of the Indian Constitution states that "within ten years of the promulgation of the Constitution, free and compulsory education shall be provided to all children up to the age of fourteen." Even after adopting this provision for 50 years, we have been unable to accomplish our aim. The National Policy of Education (NPE) declared in 1986 accelerated the mission of providing education to all children in this age group.

While the Indian government, in collaboration with state governments,has made notable advancements in various educational metrics, the ultimate objective of ensuring universal access to high-quality education has not yet been achieved. It is believed that a specific provision should be included in the Constitution's Part dealing with Fundamental Rights to accomplish this purpose.

2# The Constitution (Eighty-third Amendment) Bill, 1997 was introduced in Parliament with the intention of inserting a new article, namely, Article 21A, which grants all children in the age range of 6 to 14 years the right to free and compulsory education. The said Bill was examined by the Parliamentary Standing Committee on Human Resource Development, and the Law Commission of India covered the issue in its 165th Report.

3# The following proposed changes to Parts III, IV, and IVA of the Constitution are being made after consideringthe findings of the Law Commission of India and the recommendations of the Standing Committee of Parliament.

4# After the passage of the Constitution (Ninety-third Amendment) Bill of 2001, a law will be introduced in Parliament to provide for free and compulsory education for children between the ages of 6 and 14; (b) to include a provision in Article 45 of the Constitution stating that the State shall make every effort to provide early childhood care and education to children under the age of six; (c) to amend Article 5IA of the Constitution with a view to providing that it shall be the obligation of parents to provide opportunities for education to their children.

The Bill seeks to achieve the above objects.

9.   The Constitution (101st Amendment) Act, 2016

The Indian Constitution grants the authority to both the union and the state governments to impose taxes,as specified in their respective union and state lists.

The "one nation, one tax" system was established by the 101st Constitutional Amendment Act. This act eliminates the challenges posed by the taxation systems enacted by the federal and state governments, introducing a uniform indirect taxation system across the country.

The Central Goods and Services Tax (Extension to Jammu & Kashmir) Act, 2017, is in charge of the system, which includes the union territory of Jammu and Kashmir.

This pan-India uniform indirect tax system ensures a smooth and hassle-free flow of goods throughout the country. The Goods and Services Tax, also known as 'GST', is governed by the Constitution (One Hundred and First Amendment) Act, 2016. The GST grants power to both the central and state governments for its levy and collection.

The introduction of the 101st Constitution Amendment Act in 2016 led to some amendments and the insertion of some new articles into the Constitution of India.

Salient Features of the 101st Constitution Amendment Act:

The 101st Constitution Amendment Act of 2016 encompasses the following salient features:

◊ The creation of Article 246A enables both the federal government and individual state legislatures to pass legislation governing the use of the goods and services tax (GST). Parliament is specially empowered to legislateon matters concerning interstate supplies.

◊ The Act introduces Article 269A, dealing with Integrated Goods and Services Tax (IGST) income, focusing on inter-state supplies.The rules governing IGST are outlined in the IGST Act of 2017.

◊ The inclusion of Article 279A grants the president the authority to establish a GST council comprising ministers from the union and the states. This council has the authority to suggest, obtain, or alter any rule or regulation pertaining to the goods and services tax.

◊ The amendment to Article 286 of the Constitution limits the state's ability to impose taxes on the provision of goods, services, or both when such collections occur beyond the state's borders or involve the export and import of commodities into India.

◊ The limitation on the sale or purchase of goods is now replaced by the provision of commodities or services, or both.

◊ The Union List, State List, and Concurrent List are all included in the seventh schedule. The areas on which the union government can pass legislation are included in the Union List. The state government, on the other hand, has the power to enact laws on the ranges indicated in the State List, and both the union and the state governments have the power to do so in the jurisdictions mentioned in the Concurrent List.

The Union List gives the union government the authority to impose excise taxes on the production of natural gas, aviation turbine fuel, high-speed diesel, motor spirit and petroleum crude.

The state government can impose taxes on these five petroleum products, extending this authority to sales in foreign or interstate trade or commerce, as per the State List.

◊ If the state suffers revenue loss due to the implementation of the GST, it can seek relief in compensation from the centre. It is valid for up to 5 years under the Goods and Services (Compensation to States) Act of 2017.

Objectives of GST:

A list of objectives for the implementation of GST are as follows:

◊ **Create a Common Market:**

The primary objective of GST is to establish a common market with a uniform tax rate across India.

◊ **Eliminate Double Taxation:**

GST eliminates the issue of prior taxes for the same transaction through the provision of input tax credits.

◊ **Boost Exports:**

GST aims to enhance exports by providing refunds on the taxes collected on inputs, ensuring no tax burden on exported goods.

◊ **Increase Taxpayer Base and Revenue:**

The implementation of GST seeks to bring more taxpayers into the system, thereby expanding the tax base and increasing overall revenue.

◊ **Simplify Procedures:**

GST simplifies the application and tax return procedures by introducing common forms and providing an online payment gateway for tax payments and form submissions.

◊ **Unified IT System - GSTN:**

The Goods and Services Network (GSTN) is a unified information technology system designed to facilitate the seamless operation of GST.

What does the Seventh Schedule State?

The seventh schedule deals with the distribution of powers of legislature between the union and states. The schedule defines and specifies the allocation of powers and functions between the union and states. This distribution of subjects is based on Articles 245 and 246 of the Constitution of India.

Article 245 of the constitution defines the extent of the laws by the parliament and the state legislatures and states that *'the parliament can legislate or make laws for whole or any part of India, while the state legislature can make laws for the whole or any part of the state.'*

According to the legislation, laws passed by parliament cannot be declared unlawful merely because they involve extraterritorial activities. The laws enacted by both the parliament and state legislaturesfall under Article 246 of the Constitution,whichseparates the subjects on which the federal government and state legislatures may pass legislation.

List I (Union List):

◊   Subject to legislative action by the parliament.

List II (State List):

◊   Subject to legislative action by the states.

List III (Concurrent List):

◊   Grants both the parliament and state legislature the authority to enact laws on the listed topics. This allows states flexibility, as laws enacted by the parliament on a particular topic can be adjusted to meet state needs. In case of objectionable state laws, the parliament holds the authority to overturn them.

The 42nd Amendment Act of 1976 transferred five subjects to the Concurrent List from the State List,including:

◊ Forest

◊ Education

◊ Protection of wild animals & birds

◊ Administration of justice

◊ Weights and measurements

These subjects get allocated under three lists. These are:-

◊ Union List (List I)

◊ State List (List II)

◊ Concurrent List (List III)

The Union List covers subjects under the scope of the Union legislature. These are topics regulated exclusively by the Parliament. The Union List includes 98 issues (up from 97 initially) on which the Parliament may pass laws.

The State List addresses the authority and responsibilities granted to the states. The topics included under the State List are permitted for the states to handle. The State List now has 61 topics,reduced from the previous 66.

According to the Concurrent List, legislation on the topics listed may be passed by both the national and state legislatures. There are a total of 52 topics listed in the Concurrent List (up from 47 initially). These issues fall within the combined jurisdiction of the federal and state governments.

Types of GST:

The 101st Constitution Amendment Act led to the introduction of four types of GST for governing taxation system in India:-

- ◊ State Goods and Services Tax (SGST
- ◊ Central Goods and Services Tax (CGST)
- ◊ Integrated Goods and Services Tax (IGST)
- ◊ Union Territory Goods and Services Tax (UGST)

State Goods and Services Tax (SGST):

SGST is charged by the state government on intrastate sales of goods and services.The state government charges a sales tax. The state receives revenue when people buy products and services within the state. SGST has replaced previous taxes, including Value Added Tax (VAT), luxury tax, entertainment tax, octroi tax, lottery tax, and purchase tax.

Central Goods and Services Tax (CGST):

CGST is applied to all intrastate purchases of products and services by the central government. The Central Goods and Services Tax Act of 2017 governs this tax and the revenue collected from CGST goes to the federal government. Both the federal and state governments have agreed on the appropriate percentage of tax for relevant intra-state sales, not exceeding 14%. CGST has replaced entry tax, service tax, special extra customs duty, additional excise duty, and central excise duty.

Integrated Goods and Services Tax (IGST):

IGST is levied on interstate transactions for goods and services. The Integrated Goods and Services Tax Act of 2017 establishes the rules for IGST, which applies to both imports and exports. The revenue collected from IGST is split equally between the national and state governments, as agreed upon.

Union Territory Goods and Services Tax (UTGST):

UTGST is a tax imposed on the sale of goods and services within a particular union territory. Governed by the Union Territory Goods and Services Act, 2017, it is imposed in addition to the CGST. Similar to how the SGST is applicable to intra-state delivery of goods and services, it is also applicable to union territories.

The Union Territories subject to UTGST include the Andaman and Nicobar Islands, Chandigarh, Dadra and Nagar Haveli & Daman and Diu, Lakshadweep, Jammu and Kashmir, and Ladakh.

For the Union Territories of the National Capital Territory of Delhi and Puducherry, SGST is applicable according to their legislative provisions.

Division of the GST System:

The 101st Constitution Amendment legislation led to the division of the GST system into CGST, SGST, and IGST. The intra-state supply of goods and services is subject to CGST, SGST, and IGST, whereas the inter-state supply of goods and services is subject to IGST.

The concept of "one nation, one tax" underlies GST, consolidating all existing central and state taxes into a single tax. This replaces multiple indirect taxes previously imposed by the federal and state governments.

GST is divided into three categories—CGST, SGST, and IGSTto facilitate the easy distribution of tax among the federal government and state governments. This division ensures the efficient allocation of funds to the states, unifying the tax system.

Conclusion:

A new universal indirect taxation system is being implemented as part of the 101st Constitution Amendment Act of 2016. The amendment offers customers a clear tax structure based on the value of the goods and services they are using.

To ensure effective implementation and the allocation of fund between the federal government and state governments, GST is categorized into four tax brackets. The 101st Constitution Amendment Act sets GST rates at 5%, 12%, 18%, and 28%. The maximum rate for IGST is capped at 40%,while CGST has an upper limit of 20%. Certain goods and services, as well as specific transactions, are exempt from GST. Exemptions include gifts from employers to employees, agricultural services like harvesting, renting or leasing machinery, services provided by courts and tribunals, and the sale of land/building as per para 5(b) of Schedule II.

Under the GST regime, input tax credits are available in subsequent stages of value addition, making it taxable at the last stage of value addition.

10. The Constitution (103rd Amendment) Act, 2019

Key Highlights of the 103rd Constitution Amendment Act:

In response to a Public Interest Litigation (PIL) requesting the Supreme Court's intervention to implement the 10% Economically Weaker Sections (EWS) quota in Tamil Nadu and Karnataka without interfering with the current reservation framework, which includes the Scheduled Castes (SC), Scheduled Tribes (ST), Backward Classes (BC), and Most Backward Classes (MBC).

The 10% reservation under the Amendment Act is an addition to the existing 10% reservation. Instead of affecting or restricting anyone's fundamental right to equality, it provides equitable representation and involvement for the EWS.

The Centre informed the Supreme Court that it has no authority to determine the reservation policies of any state governments. The reservation under Articles 15(6) and 16(6) must be decided by the affected state governments.

Background of 103 Constitution Amendment Act:

The Supreme Court issued a notice to the Centre about a PIL urging the court to instruct Karnataka and Tamil Nadu to implement a 10% quota in jobs and education forEWS as per the 103rd Constitutional (Amendment) Act of 2019. The argument presented highlighted that neither Tamil Nadu nor Karnataka had implemented the amendment.

It further pointed out that,in comparison to Karnataka, which reserves 70% of employment and school seats for SC, ST, BC, and MBC individuals, Tamil Nadu only reserves 69% of such positions and seats.

The 2019 Constitutional (103rd Amendment) Act:

The amendment enabled reservation for economically disadvantaged individuals in the unreserved category by adding Articles 15 and 16 to the Constitution.

Additionally, it was passed to assist the underprivileged who were excluded from the policy of 50% reservation for SCs, STs, and Socially and Educationally Backward Classes (SEBC). It gives the Centre and the States the authority to make exceptions to the social norms.

State governments must pass this federal law for local implementation since it impacts areas (employment and education) over which both the states and the federal government have control.

Examining the 103 Constitution Amendment Act:

In the process of amending the Constitution, the challenge was to adhere to the requirements of the basic structural concept. The Supreme Court, in the case of Mr. Balaji v. the State of Mysore,concluded that exceeding a 50% quota would indicate dominance over Section 16(1) of the Constitution,as it was well-established that reservations should be kept to a maximum of 50%. The 10% reservation was introduced by the Indian government for the country's lowest 10% of citizens. However, it was eliminated following the Indira Sawhney v. Union of India case.

These choices were all made keeping in mind the law and regulations, ensuring that the basic structural philosophy was not violated. The amendment seems to just provide for a 10% reservation without expressly requiring it to be50% in Articles 15(4), 15(5), and 16(4) of the Constitution. Therefore, any objection based on a violation of the basic structural principle is rejected. Youth for Equality filed a writ case, claiming that the revision appears to go against the fundamental idea of the structure.

Two additional petitions have been submitted by solicitors Pawan and Deepak. Given that the amendment was created with equality in mind, it is difficult to see how the reservation could be said to be incompatible with equality and the fundamentals of the system.

Note:

The Supreme Court, in the case of Kesavananda Bharati v. the State of Kerala, made it clear that no legislation can be published in the Indian Gazette that undermines or harms the underlying principles of the Indian Constitution. It might be claimed that by inserting Articles 15(6) and 16(6), the 103rd Amendment was appropriately written and successfully combated socioeconomic and educational inequality.

Provision of Article 370

A Constitution Bench of the Supreme Court affirmed the President of India's authority to revoke Article 370 of the Indian Constitution on December 11, 2023, with a majority decision. As a result of this abrogation in August 2019, the former state of Jammu & Kashmir was deprived of its special privileges and split into the Union Territories of J&K and Leh. According to the Supreme Court, Article 370 was merely a stopgap meant to ease the former princely state's admission to the Union of India during a period of intense internal conflict and external attack.

◊   The judgement was passed by a five-judge constitution bench comprising Chief Justice of India DY Chandrachud, Justices Sanjay Kishan Kaul, Sanjiv Khanna, BR Gavai, and Surya Kant.

◊   The SC said that steps should be taken to conduct elections in the assembly by September 30, 2024.

◊   The Supreme Court did not accept the argument of petitioners that the Union government cannot take actions of irreversible consequences in Jammu & Kashmir during President's Rule (the abrogation was done during President's Rule).

◊   The Supreme Court also said that Jammu and Kashmir did not retain an element of sovereignty after joining India.

Article 370 – Introduction

The main thrust of Article 370 was that the State Legislature had the authority to ratify Central laws by enacting a separate act, rather than the laws of the Parliament automatically applying to the former State of J&K.

◊   Article 370 is a constitutional provision that granted Jammu and Kashmir its special status.

◊   The provision was incorporated in Part XXI of the Constitution: Temporary, Transitional, and Special Provisions.

» As evident from the title of the Part, it was supposed to be a temporary provision, and its applicability was projected to last until the formulation and adoption of the State's constitution.

◊ It restricted the Parliament's legislative powers with respect to the state of J&K.

On November 27, 1963, Pandit Jawaharlal Nehru stated on the Lok Sabha floor that Article 370 had deteriorated, and the erosion process was still ongoing. A year later, on December 4, 1964, on the floor of the Lok Sabha, the then-home minister Gulzari Lal Nanda declared, "Article 370 is a tunnel to take the Constitution of India to Jammu and Kashmir." He added that whether it is retained or not won't really matter in the end because all that will be left is the shell, empty of anything inside.

Just ten years after the Indian Constitution was enacted, these two declarations from two of the nation's most powerful leaders reveal much about the weakening of Article 370. The Constitutional Application Order of 1950 marked the beginning of the process, and several discussions between the Central government and the State government followed. These discussions resulted in the Delhi Agreement of 1952, which agreed to apply to the State of J&K a number of subjects not included in the Instrument of Accession. Here are a few of them:

◊ Appointment of the head of State.

◊ Persons having domicile in the State of J&K shall be Citizens of India.

◊ Fundamental Rights

◊ Jurisdiction of Supreme Court

◊ National Flag

◊ Financial Integration

◊ Emergency Powers

Presidential Orders:

Under Article 370 of the Constitution of India, the President has the power of issuing orders for the application of provisions of the Constitution of India with modifications, exceptions and amendments in the provisions. And this power has been upheld in several cases by the Supreme Court, e.g., in P. L. **Lakhanpal vs the State of J&K.**

As already said, for the application of other provisions of the Constitution of India to the State of J&K, the only mode available was the Constitutional Application Order. And the same was to be done with the consultation and concurrence of the State Government. The Presidential Orders, broadly speaking, deal with the following subject matters:

◊ Enhancing the jurisdiction of the Parliament to enact laws in the State of J&K out of the Union List.

◊ Laws relating to an increase or decrease in the area of the State.

◊ Making provisions for the return of the permanent residents of the State who migrated to the territories included in Pakistan under permit for settlement.

◊ Providing for constitutional protection to the laws relating to permanent residents of the state, their special rights and privileges, employment under Government, acquisition of immovable property, settlement in the State, scholarships.

◊ Earmarking the number of seats in the House of the People, excluding the area under the occupation of Pakistan.

◊ Provision for delimitation of Parliament Constituencies.

◊ Transfer of judges from the High Court of J&K or to the said Court.

◊ Exclusion of the State List.

◊ Provision as regards the decision affecting the disposition of the State of J&K.

◊ Acquisition and requisition of immovable property on behalf of and at the expense of the Union.

◊ Provision relating to the use of the official language of the Union and in the proceedings before the Supreme Court.

◊ Provisions for the proclamation of emergency.

◊ Provisions for non-application of the amendments carried out by the Parliament of India in the Constitution of India.

◊ Provision for the Governor and the Election Commission.

In the year 1954, the Constitutional Application Order 1950 was renamed as the Constitutional Application Order 1954, and its issuance was the first infringement on the constitutional autonomy of the State of J&K. It culminated with the issuance of the Constitution (Application to J&K) Order, 2019. Article 370 itself was used to make it weak after remaining on the Constitution book for 70 years.

Facts on Article 370:

Article 370 – Temporary provisions with respect to the State of Jammu and Kashmir

1# Notwithstanding anything in this Constitution:

i. The provisions of Article 238 shall not apply in relation to the State of Jammu and Kashmir;

ii. The power of Parliament to make laws for the said State shall be limited to:

a# Those items on the Union List and the Concurrent List that the President, after consulting with the State Government, declares to correspond to the items listed in the Instrument of Accession governing the State's admission to the Dominion of India as the subjects on which the State's legislature may enact laws;

b# Other matters in the aforementioned Lists that the President may, by order, give Explanation for, with the State Government's consent. In this article, "Government of the State" refers to the individual designated by the President as the Maharaja of Jammu and Kashmir, acting on the Council of Ministers' advice while in office in accordance with the Maharajas Proclamation dated March 5, 1948;

c# The provisions of Article 1 and of this article shall apply in relation to that State;

d# Such of the other provisions of this Constitution shall apply in relation to that State subject to such exceptions and modifications as the President may, by order, specify: With the caveat that no such order pertaining to the subjects included in the State's Instrument of Accession mentioned in paragraph 1 of sub-clause (b) may be made without first consulting the State government.Additionally, no such order pertaining to subjects other than those mentioned in the previous proviso may be made without the government's approval.

2# If the concurrence of the Government of the State referred to in paragraph 2 of sub-clause (b) of clause (1) or in the second proviso to sub-clause (d) of that clause be given before the Constituent Assembly for the purpose of framing the Constitution of the State is convened, it shall be placed before such Assembly for such a decision as it may take thereon.

3# Despite the aforementioned provisions of this article, the President may, by means of public announcement, proclaim that this article will either no longer be in effect or will only be in effect with the exceptions and adjustments he deems necessary, starting on a date of his choosing.The proviso is that the **recommendation of the Constituent Assembly of the State referred to in clause (2)** shall be necessary before the President issues such a notification.

Application of 370:

◊ But on January 25, 1957, the State's constituent parliament disbanded without suggesting that Article 370 be repealed or amended, leaving the future of the clause uncertain.

◊ Subsequently, the Supreme Court of India and the High Court of Jammu and Kashmir ruled that the provision had gained permanent status.

◊ This suggested that the state government just has to be "consulted" in order for central legislation to be applied to it on matters covered by the Instrument of Accession.

◊ Nevertheless, the "concurrence" of the state government was required in order to apply central legislation to subjects other than communications, foreign affairs, and defense.

Jammu and Kashmir Constitution:

◊ **Article 3– Relationship of the State with the Union of India:-** The State of Jammu and Kashmir is and shall be an integral part of the Union of India.

◊ There is no assertion of sovereignty in the Preamble to the J&K Constitution, but it is also explicitly acknowledged that its goal is "to further define the existing relationship of the state with the Union of India as its integral part thereof."

Constitution (Application to Jammu and Kashmir) Order, 2019

- ◊ (1)This Order may be called the Constitution (Application to Jammu and Kashmir) Order, 2019.

    - » (2) It shall come into force at once, and shall thereupon supersede the Constitution (Application to Jammu and Kashmir) Order, 1954 as amended from time to time.

- ◊ The State of Jammu and Kashmir shall be subject to all the provisions of the Constitution, as amended from time to time; the following exclusions and amendments shall be subject to such application:-

To article 367, there shall be added the following clause, namely:-

- ◊ (4) For the purposes of this Constitution as it applies in relation to the State of Jammu and Kashmir-

    - » References to this Constitution or to its provisions shall be construed as references to the Constitution or the provisions thereof as applied in relation to the said State;

    - » References to the person for the time being recognized by the President on the recommendation of the Legislative Assembly of the State as the Sadar-i-Riyasat of Jammu and

Kashmir, acting on the advice of the Council of Ministers of the State for the time being in office, shall be construed as references to the Governor of Jammu and Kashmir;

» References to the Government of the said State shall be construed as including references to the Governor of Jammu and Kashmir acting on the advice of his Council of Ministers; and

» In the proviso to clause (3) of Article 370 of this Constitution, the expression "Constituent Assembly of the State referred to in clause (2)" shall read "Legislative Assembly of the State".

Has Article 370 been scrapped?

◊ Article 370 has not been repealed by the presidential order that the Indian president has signed.

◊ However, the special status of Jammu & Kashmir has been revoked, citing this very article.

◊ Article 370 is, therefore, firmly entrenched in the law book.

◊ Put differently, the government's action allows Jammu & Kashmir to fully benefit from the Indian Constitution. Jammu & Kashmir was previously under the exclusive purview of a small number of rules related to communication, foreign relations, and defense.

What is the status of Article 35-A?

Since the Fundamental Rights chapter has been expanded by the **Presidential Order on August 5,** which extended all the Constitution's provisions to Kashmir, some of the Article 35-A's discriminatory elements may no longer be compliant with established regulations.

As a result, the President may also rule that this is not relevant.

CHAPTER 4

Twenty Landmark Cases that changed the Indian Legal System

1. Judgment on The Basic Structure Doctrine – Kesavananda Bharati v. State of Kerala (1973)

Facts of the Case:

Kesavananda Bharati, the leader of the Edneer Mutt, a congregation in Kerala's Kasaragod District. He had a few parcels of land that were registered in his name. A section of the sect's land, which belonged to Keshvananda Bharti, faced by the government under the Land Reforms Amendment Act approved by Kerala's state government in 1969.

In his 1970 appeal to the Supreme Court, he invoked various articles of the Indian Constitution,including Articles 25 (Right to practise and propagate religion), 26 (Right to manage religious affairs), 14 (Right to equality), 19(1)(f) (Freedom to Acquire Property), and 31 (Right to Administer Religious Matters). While the court was still considering the petition, the Kerala Government approved another law, the Kerala Land Reforms (Amendment) Act, in 1971.

Main Issues of the case:

◊ Is the 24th Amendment to the Constitution (Amendment) Act of 1971 constitutionally valid?

◊ Is the 25th Amendment to the Constitution (Amendment) Act of 1972 constitutionally valid?

◊ The degree to which Parliament can use its constitutional amendment powers.

◊ What constitutes the "Basic Structure"?

Judgment:

1# The Supreme Court, by a 7:6 majority, overturned the Golaknath Case judgement, in favour of the government's authority to amend fundamental rights under Articles 13(2) and 368(3) and the constitution under Article 368 without altering the Constitution's core principles.

2# Section 2(a) and 2(b) of the 25th Amendment and the first half of section 3 were deemed constitutionally valid. Likewise, it was agreed that the 24th and 29th amendments were genuine.

3# The majority of judges declared that Article 31C of the Constitution, which was added by the 25th Amendment, is invalid with regard to the 25th Amendment. However, Justice Khanna, on the other hand, found that the first part of Article 31C was lawful, but the second part was invalid, contradicting Justice Reddy's conclusion that both the portions of Article 31C are legitimate.

4# The "basic structure doctrine" was advanced by Justice Hans Raj Khanna, who concluded that the Indian Constitution has some fundamental components that cannot be altered or removed by legislative modifications. The idea, he said, is represented in some of the fundamental elements of democracy, such as sovereignty, freedom, secularism, judicial scrutiny, separation of powers, etc., even if it is not explicitly articulated anywhere. According to him, the doctrine only applies to constitutional amendments that could undermine or alter the fundamental philosophical principles of the original constitution. Therefore, any legislation that violates the essential structural principle may be declared void by the Supreme Court.

2.   Judgment on The Right of Personal Liberty – Maneka Gandhi v. Union of India (1978)

Facts of the Case:

Maneka Gandhi, the petitioner, was a journalist whose passport was granted in accordance with the Passport Act of 1967 on June 1st. On July 2nd, 1977, the Regional Passport Officer in New Delhi sent the petitioner a letter requesting the return of her passport. When questioned about the cancellation reasons, the Ministry of External Affairs cited "public interest" and refused to answer any questions.

According to the petitioner, the seizure of her passport violated her fundamental rights, specifically under Articles 14 (Right to Equality), 19 (Right to Freedom of Speech & Expression), and 21 (Right to Life and Liberty).Consequently, she filed a writ petition under Article 32 of the Indian Constitution.

Additionally, the petitioner was allegedly required to attend proceedings before a Commission of Inquiry, based on a document forged by the defendant.

Main Issues of the Case:

◊ What does the Indian Constitution's provision of fundamental rights to people mean in practise?

◊ Whether or not the 'Right to Travel Abroad' is protected by Article 21.

◊ What is the relationship between the rights provided by India's Constitution Articles 14, 19, and 21?

◊ Defining the extent of the word "procedure established by law."

◊ Is Section 10(3)(c) of the Passport Act of 1967 an actual law, and if so, does it violate fundamental rights?

Judgment:

On January 25, 1978, this landmark judgement was delivered, bringing irreversible changes to the Indian Constitution. As stated in the Preamble, this judgement considerably increased the scope of Article 21, and transformed India into a welfare state. Except for a few points where several justices concurred, the seven-judge panel came to a unanimous decision.

The court's key conclusions were as follows:

1# Although Article 21 refers to "procedure established by law" rather than "due process of law," the court, in this landmark case, ruled that the procedure must be free from arbitrariness and irrationality.

2# The court overruled the Gopalan case, concluding that every legislation must meet the requirements outlined in Articles 14, 19, and 21 and that there is a special link between those provisions.

3# The court decided that the term "personal liberty" should not be interpreted in a restrictive and rigid meaning. According to the court, personal liberty must be defined in a broad and liberal meaning. As a result, Article 21 has been given a broad meaning.

4# The right to travel abroad, as established in Satwant Singh, falls within the scope of Article 21.

5# Section 10(3)(c) (g) of the Passport Act of 1967 does not violate either Article 21 or Article 19(1)(a) or 19(1)(b). The court further stated that the 1967 measure did not violate Article 14 As the mentioned clause allows for an opportunity to be heard.

6# Sections 10(3)(c) and 10(5) are administrative orders, according to the court, and thus subject to dispute on the grounds of mala fide, unreasonableness, denial of natural justice, and ultra vires.

7# The court further advised the government to disclose reasons in every case and to only utilize the prerogative of Section 10(5) of the 1967 statute on rare occasions.

3. Judgment on The Right to Livelihood – Olga Tellis v. Bombay Municipal Corporation (1985)

Facts of the Case:

A.R. Antulay, the then-chief minister of Maharashtra, declared in 1981 that those living on Mumbai's streets and pavements would be forcibly removed from their homes and sent elsewhere, most likely outside the city.

The petitioners argued that Article 32 of the Constitution, which is protected by Article 21 of the Constitution, includes the right to livelihood as a component of the right to life. Olga Tellis, was one of the petitioners, who contended that the eviction order was unreasonable and unfair since it did not offer any alternative housing options for the people living on the streets.

Furthermore, petitioners claimed that Articles 14, 19, and 21 of the Indian Constitution are violated by Sections 312, 313, and 314 of the Bombay Municipal Corporation Act.

Main Issues of the Case:

◊ Whether Article 21 of the Constitution encompasses the right to life and livelihood.

◊ Whether sections 312, 313, and 314 of the Bombay Municipal Corporation Act are constitutional.

◊ Question of Fundamental Rights Waiver or Estoppels Against Fundamental Rights.

◊ Whether or not people who live on the sidewalk are considered trespassers under the IPC.

Judgment:

The court held that any impairment of one's right to a livelihood or means of sustenance is unlawful since the right to life also includes that right. It demonstrated the justices' humanistic view and the court's active position.

The court made the following ruling in this case:

1# No one has the right to encroach upon public trails, sidewalks, or any other public space.

2# In the facts of this case, section 314 of the Bombay Municipality Act is not irrational.

3# Slums that have been in place for at least 20 years shall not be demolished unless the property is needed for public use, and in such cases, other locations must be allocated.

4# Resettlement should be given priority.

4. Judgment on the Absolute Liability Principle – M.C. Mehta v. Union of India(1987)

Facts of the Case:

A social activist lawyer named M.C. Mehta filed a writ petition calling for the closure of Shriram Industries, which manufactured dangerous chemicals and was situated in Kirti Nagar, a densely populated area.

On the 4th and 6th of December 1985, an oil gas leak from one of the petition's units happened while it was still in operation, resulting in the death of one of the petitioner's supporters and posing health risks to others. This incident made me think of the Bhopal gas catastrophe.

M.C. Mehta requested the closure and relocation of the Shriram Caustic Chlorine and Sulphuric Acid Plant, located in a heavily populated area of Delhi, and moved in a Public Interest Litigation (PIL) under Articles 21 and 32 of the Constitution.

The Inspector of Factories and the Commissioner (Factories) issued separate orders on December 8 and 24, 1985, respectively, to shut down the factories. This occurrence took place only a few months before the Environment (Protection) Act went into effect, and therefore constitutes a driving factor for enacting such legislation.

In the Shriram Food and Fertiliser Industry case, the Supreme Court of India issued six reported rulings, four of which were handed down before the Environment (Protection) Act, 1986 was approved and the day it went into force.

Main Issues:

◊ Is it permissible for such hazardous enterprises to operate in such areas?

◊ Is there any way to regulate them if they are permitted to work in such areas?

◊ The extent of the liability and the amount of compensation to be paid must be established.

Judgment:

In this case, the following decisions were made:

1# In tort law, the idea of strict responsibility or absolute culpability was formed.

2# The court concluded that the fertiliser plant could not operate in such close proximity to habitation due to the risk involved, leading to the relocation of the firm. The "deep pocket" hypothesis was also proven.

3# This decision also marked the beginning of a period of important legislative advancement in India. A totally new chapter that included exact quotes from the judgement was added to the 1948 Factory Act.

4# A programme for pollution management was established, and the Public Liability Insurance Act was passed.

5# Additionally, the Policy for Pollution Control Abatement and the Environment Protection Act were also passed into law.

5. Judgment on Sexual Harassment of Women at Workplace – Vishakha v. State of Rajasthan (1997)

Facts of the Case:

As a social worker, Bhanwari Devi participated in a Rajasthan state government programme to address the problem of child marriage. During the demonstration, she tried her utmost to stop the child marriage of a female newborn in one of Ramakant Gujjar's households. Despite a lot of protest, the marriage was successfully ended.

The sub-divisional officer (SDO) and the deputy superintendent of police (DSP) stopped the aforementioned marriage. Nevertheless, the wedding was held, and no police action was taken as a result. Later, people learned that Bhanwari Devi's actions were what led to the police visits. Bhanwari Devi and her family thus becamethe target of a boycott. Bhanwari lost her job in the midst of it.

Ramakant Gujjar and his five men gang-raped her in front of her husband in 1992 to exact vengeance. The police department attempted to dissuade her from pursuing the case on various grounds, but she persisted and filed a complaint against the accused. However, she was exposed to extreme treatment by female police attendants, to the point that her lehenga was demanded from her to get proof, and she was left with nothing except her husband's blood-stained dhoti. The trial court found the accused not guilty, but she never gave up hope. Seeing her tenacity, all-female social workers came to her defence. They collectively submitted a writ suit to the Supreme Court of India under the name "Vishakha" to create guidelines to prevent sexual harassment at work.The Supreme Court was consulted for this purpose.

Main Issues of the Case:

◊ Is the employer obligated to address instances of sexual harassment at the workplace by any of its workers or employees?

◊ The need for formal guidelines to deal with workplace sexual harassment incidents.

Judgment:

The Vishakha v. The State of Rajasthan case resulted in the Supreme Court issuing the Vishakha Guidelines (1997).These guidelines laid the foundation for the Sexual Harassment of Women at Workplace (Prevention, Prohibition, and Redressal) Act, 2013.The act mandated institutions across the country to maintain an Internal Complaints Committee (ICC), consisting of 10 or more employees led by a female.

Broadly, the following was underlined:

1# Sexual harassment of women is a gross violation of their fundamental rights, including under Articles 14, 19, and 21.

2# A robust mechanism was established for the redressal of complaints. For this purpose, a complaints' committee was directed to be set up and NGOs were involved.

6. Judgment on Passive Euthanasia – Aruna Ramachandra Shanbaug v. Union of India (2011)

Facts of the Case:

Aruna Ramchandra Shanbaug was the nursing in-charge at Parel's King Edward Memorial Hospital. One day, a hospital sweeper assaulted her and pulled her back with a dog chain around her neck. This catastrophe irreversibly harmed her brain, causing her to enter a persistent vegetative state (PVS).

Pinki Virani, an activist and journalist, petitioned the Supreme Court under Article 32 of the constitution, arguing that since she was terminally ill and had no possibility of recovery, she should be let to pass away peacefully. This was not acceptable. She held this position for 42 years before passing away in 2015.

Main Issues:

◊ Is it ethical to discontinue life support equipment and procedures for a person in a persistent vegetative state (PVS)?

◊ Should the wishes of a patient who has expressed a desire to forgo life-sustaining treatments in the case of ineffective therapy or PVS be respected?

◊ If the patient has not previously requested the withholding or withdrawal of life-sustaining systems, can the patient's family or next of kin submit such a request?

Judgment:

After consulting with doctors, the Supreme Courtconcluded that her brain was not dead, and she was capable of breathing and experiencing emotions despite being in a PVS. It was held to be unjustifiable to take her life against her wishes.

Simultaneously,the judgement recognised the right to die and legalised passive euthanasia, also known as mercy killing. To avoid abuse, various restrictions were placed on this. A detailed protocol was established and called for:

1# High Court clearance after following the proper procedure,

2# Evaluation of the opinions of three reputable and qualified physicians,

3# Approval by a bench of two judges, and

4# Notification to the patient's close family members.

7. Judgment on Disqualification of Convicted Representatives – Lily Thomas v. Union of India (2013)

Facts of the Case:

Adv. Lily Thomas filed a writ petition in the Supreme Court in 2005 to challenge Section 8(4) of the Representation of the People Act, which shields politicians who have been convicted of crimes from being disqualified from running for office because appeals against their convictions are still pending in the appellate courts.

Even though the petitioners' plea was initially rejected, a Supreme Court bench made up of Justices AK Patnaik and SJ Mukhopadhaya gave a ruling in July 2013 after nine years of trial.

Main Issues:

◊   Whether Parliament has the power to carry out Section 8(4) of the Act was the first issue raised in the case.

◊   Second, whether Section 8(4) of the Act, which permitted members of a certain class to keep membership while being convicted of a crime, violated the terms of the Indian Constitution and contradicted the intentions and purposes of its writers.

Judgment:

According to the decision, any Members of Parliament (MPs) or Members of Legislative Assembly (MLAs), elected or unelected, found guilty in a criminal case by a trial court would be immediately disqualified, and the section 8(4) saving clause would not be applicable. This affectedapproximately 5000 elected officials.

The court held that:

1# The Constitution is violated by Section 8(4).

2# "Subsection (4) of Section 8 of the Act is ultra vires the Constitution" because the Parliament lacked the authority to enact it.

3# Both candidates and representatives (members) may be disqualified for the same reasons.

4# Any serving MP, MLA, or MLC found guilty under subsections 1, 2, or 3 of section 8 is immediately disqualified.

8. Judgment on The Right to Self-identification of The Third Gender – NALSA v. Union of India (2014)

Facts of the Case:

In India, the transgender community exhibits a broad spectrum of gender nonconformity. Within this range are hermaphrodites, pre- and post-operative transsexuals, and transvestites.

The petition, which was filed in 2012 by a non-governmental organisation on behalf of the Kinnar transgender community, demanded a formal recognition of the petitioner's gender identity,challenging the gender assigned to them at birth. The petitioner claimed that failure to do so violated Articles 14 and 21 of the Indian Constitution.

The Additional Solicitor General, who represented the government, admitted that the predicament was a serious social issue. He disclosed to the court that the government had previously established an expert committee to look into various problems facing the transgender community.

Main Issues:

◊ Whether a person born as a man with a mainly feminine inclination (or vice versa) has the right to be recognized as a female of his or her choice, particularly when such a person undergoes a surgical procedure to alter his or her sex as a female.

◊ Do transgender people, who are neither men nor females, have the right to be labeled as a "third gender"?

◊ Whether the non-recognition of various gender identities violates Articles 14 and 21 of the Constitution?

Judgment:

To defend and protect the rights of transgender people guaranteed by India's constitution, it was ruled that:

1# Hijras and Eunuchs must be recognized as "third gender" alongside binary gender.

2# Transgender individuals have the right to determine their own gender identity.

3# They must be given preference in admission to public educational institutions and employment and must be considered as socially and educationally backward classes.

4# They are entitled to access government support programmes.

5# Facilities for addressing their psychological and physical health issues must be offered.

9. Judgment on Freedom of Speech and Expression Over the Internet – Shreya Singhal v. Union of India (2015)

Facts of the Case:

In the year 2012, Shaheen Dhada and Rinu Srinivasan were detained by the Mumbai policein response to a call for a strike (bandh) by Shiv Sena supporters in Maharashtra,protesting the passing of the party's president, Bal Thackery. The petitioners were accused of posting their comments on Facebook, which caused a great deal of uproar from the general public. The petitioners, who used the public interest defence, filed a writ petition under Article 32 of the Constitution, claiming that section 66A of the IT Act 2000 violated their right to freedom of speech and expression.

Main Issues:

◊ Whether the IT Act's Sections 66-A, 69-A, and 79 are constitutionally valid?

◊ Is Section 66A of the IT Act a violation of the basic right to freedom of expression and speech?

Judgment:

1# The Court determined that section 66A of the IT Act is an arbitrary rule that undermines the right to free speech and expression online for citizens and is in derogation of Article 19(1)(a).

2# The Court continued by stating that Section 66A cannot be justified in light of the restrictions on free speech and expression established in Article 19(2), such as those related to public order, defamation, incitement to commit an offence, decency, and morality.

3# The Court also found that the language used in Section 66A was ambiguous, vague, and open-ended. As used under the clause, words like "annoying," "inconvenience," and "grossly offensive" do not allude to a specific crime, making it unclear to both law enforcement and the general public what is and is not permitted.

4# While Section 66A was struck down, the constitutional legality of sections 69A and 79 was affirmed because the regulations created under them dealt with intermediary liability and were drafted with many protections.

10. Judgment on the Right to Privacy as a Fundamental Right – Justice K.S. Puttaswamy (Retd.) v. Union of India (2017)

Facts of the Case:

In 2012, retired High Court Judge K.S. Puttaswamy challenged the legality of the Aadhaar system concerning "the right to privacy" by filing a petition in the Supreme Court against the Union of India. The matter was brought before the Constitution Bench to determine whether the right to privacy was recognised as a separate fundamental right under the Indian Constitution, given earlier court rulings.

Main Issue:

◊ Does the Indian Constitution recognize a right to privacy as a basic right?

◊ Whether the 'Aadhaar scheme' violates privacy.

Judgment:

1# The Supreme Court of India's nine-judge panel gave a significant ruling on August 24, 2017, upholding the basic right to privacy protected by Article 21 of the Indian Constitution. In other words, it was decided that section III of the Constitution's right to privacy was a given.

2# The court supported the Aadhaar Legislation by arguing that the collection of biometric and demographic data does not violate the fundamental right to privacy because the data is limited and only used for identification purposes.

3# The Supreme Court also stated that as fundamental rights cannot be conferred or revoked by legislation and all laws and acts must comply with the Constitution, the state must, at all costs, strike a careful balance between peoples' privacy and legitimate aims.

4# The Court also clarified that the right to privacy is not absolute and is subject to the "procedure established by law". Any invasion of privacy by a state or non-state actor must pass the triple tests, which includes the following:

i.   Legitimate Aim

ii. The proportionality principle

iii. Compliance with the law

11. Citizens for the Democracy v. State of Assam

In this case, Mr. Kuldip Nayar, a renowned journalist and president of "Citizens for Democracy," brought to the attention of the Supreme Court that seven TADA detainees held in the hospital in the State of Assam were handcuffed and tied with a long rope to restrict their movement. Security personnel were stationed outside the hospital as well. Treating communication as a letter petition under Article 32 of the Indian Constitution, the Court determined that handcuffing and tying them with ropes patient prisoners housed in the hospital violates their human rights, safeguarded by both international law and domestic law.

The court clarified that when a person is detained by the police without a warrant, and the police officer determines, based on the aforementioned rules, that handcuffing the detained person is essential, he may do so up to the point at which the detainee is transported to the police station and then presented before the magistrate. Any subsequent use of restraints must be done under the orders of the magistrate.

12. National Legal Services Authority v. Union of India

In this historic decision, the Apex Court granted a petition on behalf of the nation's transgender population, and it concluded that the freedom to express one's identity in a non-binary gender was a crucial component of free speech. The court instructed the government to officially recognise the third gender so that people might choose whether to identify as male, female, or third gender.

Referring to Article 14 of the Indian Constitution, which states that "the state shall not deny to 'any person' equality before the law or the equal protection of the laws within the territory of India," it was decided that "transgender persons who are neither male nor female fall within the expression 'person' and, therefore, are entitled to legal protection under the laws in all spheres of State activity, including employment, healthcare, and education."

13. Shayara Bano v. Union of India (Triple Talaq Case)

The Honourable Supreme Court considered the appeal challenging "Triple Talaq" or "Instant Talaq," an Islamic custom that permits men to swiftly divorce their wives by uttering the word "talaq" three times. On August 22, 2017, a constitution bench comprising five justices representing various religions ruled,by a margin of 3:2, that Triple Talaq, also known as Talaq-e-Biddat, was unconstitutional. Honorable Law Minister Shri Ravi Shankar Prasad took the initiative to present the Triple Talaq Bill before the Lower House, Lok Sabha, which was passed by a majority on December 28, 2017, taking into account the opinions of the Hon. Supreme Court in the Judgement of Shayara Bano Vs. Union of India. However, the judgement has not served as a deterrent in reducing the incidences of triple talaq, according to the statement of Objects and Reasons of the Bill. "Therefore, it is felt that State action is necessary to give effect to the Supreme Court's order and to redress the grievances of victims of illegal divorce," the statement continues. It is urgently important to enact adequate laws to provide some relief for the unfortunate married Muslim women in order to stop the harassment that is still being meted out to them as a result of talaq-e-biddat.

14. Hussainara Khatoon v. The State of Bihar

In the "Hussainara Khatoon" case, Kapila Hingorani created history by filing the PIL in March 1979 and gaining the release of almost 40,000 undertrial prisoners who were being held in the jails of Bihar's Patna and Muzzafarpur. The Hussainara Khatoon case changed the Indian legal system, which, up until 1979, was only available to people directly impacted by the law or subject to punishment. Public Interest Litigations (PILs) became an established part of Indian law when the court permitted Hingorani to pursue a lawsuit in which she lacked personal locus standi (the ability to commence an action or to present in court). Since then, PILs have emerged as the ally of the oppressed and those treated unfairly by the system.

15. Indian Council for Environment Legal Action v. Union of India

The court applied the 'Polluter Pays' theory for the first time in this case. According to this theory, 'the financial costs of preventing or remedying damage caused by pollution should lie with the undertakings which cause pollution or produce the goods that cause pollution.' The Supreme Court also referenced the decision made in the M. C. Mehta v. Union of India case, which was in charge of introducing and developing the doctrine of absolute responsibility in India. According to this regulation, 'any person who engages in any inherently dangerous or hazardous activity shall be absolutely liable and shall not be entitled to plead any defence in respect of any harm caused to any person during the performance of such hazardous activity.'

16. Shreya Singhal v. Union of India

By overturning section 66A of the Information Technology Act, 2000—which allowed for the arrest of those who uploaded allegedly harmful information online—the Supreme Court upheld the right to free speech. A conviction under Section 66A carries a potential sentence of three years in prison and a fine for sending "offensive" texts via computer or any other communication device, including a mobile phone or tablet.

17. Independent Thought v. Union of India (Marital Rape of Minor Wife)

In this important ruling, the Supreme Court determined that having sex with a minor wife constitutes rape. The exemption for a husband whose wife is between 15 and 18 years old, according to the court, cannot endure and must be eliminated. Exception 2 to Section 375 of the Indian Penal Code, which excused marital rape of females between the ages of 15 and 18, was overturned by the Supreme Court when it was making the aforementioned statement.

18. M. Siddiq v. Mahant Suresh Das & Ors. (Ayodhya Case)

In its majority decision, the Supreme Court allowed for the construction of a Ram temple at the contentious site in Ayodhya and ordered the government to provide the Sunni Waqf Board with a 5-acre plot on which to erect a mosque. The Supreme Court agreed to transfer ownership of the contentious site to a trust run by the federal government, which would be in charge of all operations, including the construction of a Ram temple. The court mandated that the government purchase another parcel of land on which a mosque might be constructed while emphasising that the Babri Masjid's demolition was unlawful. The court said that the Allahabad High Court, which had divided the land between the Hindu and Muslim parties to the suit, "defied logic".

19. Puttuswamy v. Union of India (Right to Privacy is a Fundamental Right)

The Supreme Court of India declared that Article 21 of the Indian constitution protects the basic right to privacy as integral to life and liberty for Indians. The Court overturned decisions made in the M.P. Sharma case in 1958 and the Kharak Singh case in 1961, both of which said that the right to privacy is not guaranteed by the Indian Constitution. This ruling, presented in a 547-page judgement, proclaims privacy as a fundamental right.

20. The Nanavati Case

The one that allegedly brought an Indian jury trial to a close.You may be familiar with the Bollywood film Rustom, which was based on a real-life incident from the 1960s. In India, jury trials are considered to have concluded as a result of this case. Prem Ahuja, a man who supposedly had an affair with K.M. Nanavati's wife, was murdered, and Nanavati was put on trial for the crime.

◊ The petitioner, K.M. Nanavati, was a naval officer. In 1959, the wife of Nanavati confessed to her husband about her extramarital relationship with Mr. Ahuja. Nanavati shot Ahuja dead at his home out of rage with a loaded handgun. Nanavati surrendered to local authorities and was subsequently given a court date.

◊ The case was transferred to Bombay for a jury trial. With an initial 8:1 judgement, the jury found Nanavati not guilty of violating Section 302. The Session Court, in contrast, disapproved of the viewpoint and forwarded the ruling to the Bombay High Court. Nanavati was found guilty under Section 302 of the IPC by the High Court.The decision was appealed to the Supreme Court. The SC found the conviction and sentence of life imprisonment passed on him by the High Court are correct, and stated that there were absolutely no grounds for interference.

The case gained traction in the media and received widespread publicity, which is said to have influenced the jury's verdict. The episode served as the basis for various dramatised versions and films, making the case well-known to the general public. So much so that everyone is knowledgeable of the case's details.

However, what most people get wrong is that this is India's last jury trial case. The last jury trial, in fact, took place in 1973 in Calcutta!

CHAPTER 5

CONCLUSION OF IGNITED LEGAL MINDS

In the intricate tapestry of global affairs, where threads of geopolitics and strands of legal intricacies weave together, our journey through this book has been one of exploration and revelation. From the echoing corridors of power to the nuanced corridors of the law, we've navigated through a landscape shaped by history, molded by politics, and etched by the pen of jurisprudence.

The fusion of geopolitics and Indian law, examined through the lens of this comprehensive volume, reveals a dynamic interplay of forces that transcend borders and boundaries. As we reflect on the myriad topics explored within these pages, it becomes evident that understanding the complexities of our world necessitates an awareness of the interconnectedness between global power dynamics and legal frameworks.

At the heart of our exploration lies the shifting sands of geopolitics, where nations jockey for influence, resources, and strategic advantage. The rise and fall of empires, the clash of ideologies, and the pursuit of national interest have sculpted the geopolitical landscape, leaving indelible imprints on the destinies of nations. From the chessboard of international relations to the negotiation tables of diplomatic summits, the chapters unfolded a panorama of geopolitical forces shaping the destiny of not just India but the entire world.

India, a nation with a rich tapestry of history and culture, stands at the crossroads of global geopolitics. Its strategic location, burgeoning economy, and diverse population make it a key player on the international stage. The examination of India's geopolitical position within the broader context of this book elucidates the delicate dance between sovereignty and collaboration, self-interest and global responsibility.

A significant portion of our journey through these pages has delved into the legal scaffolding that underpins the Indian state. The intricate web of laws, from constitutional provisions to legislative enactments, weaves together a framework that governs the lives of its citizens. The exploration of Indian law in this volume is not merely a legal discourse but a voyage into the very soul of a nation, its values, aspirations, and the continuous effort to balance tradition with progress.

The discussion on the constitutional landscape has been particularly enlightening. The meticulous crafting of the Indian Constitution, an amalgamation of diverse voices and ideologies, reflects the aspirations of a young nation stepping into the uncharted territory of self-governance. Article 370, a constitutional provision that granted special autonomy to Jammu and Kashmir, became a focal point of our inquiry. Its abrogation in 2019 marked a significant turning point, stirring debates on constitutional propriety, federalism, and the delicate equilibrium between unity and diversity.

The interplay between geopolitics and Indian law is not merely an academic exercise, but a lived reality for millions. The chapters that unfolded the legal aspects of issues like cross-border conflicts, human rights, and environmental regulations elucidate the intricate dance between national and international legal frameworks. The examination of case studies, both historic and contemporary, underscores the dynamic nature of law as it grapples with the evolving challenges of a globalized world.

As we draw the curtains on this comprehensive exploration, it is essential to acknowledge the dynamic nature of the topics discussed. Geopolitics is not static, and legal landscapes are ever-evolving. The lessons of the past and the challenges of the present converge to shape the future. In the corridors of power and the courtrooms, decisions made today resonate through time, influencing the trajectory of nations and the lives of individuals.

In conclusion, the synthesis of geopolitics and Indian law presented in this book offers a panoramic view of the complexities inherent in the globalized world. It is a call to action, a reminder that every legal decision, every geopolitical move, has far-reaching consequences. As we step away from these pages, may we carry with us not just knowledge but a sense of responsibility — an understanding that in the realm of geopolitics and law, each of us plays a role, no matter how small, in shaping the destiny of our world.